EXPLORING AUTUMN

BOOKS BY SANDRA MARKLE

Exploring Winter
Exploring Summer
Exploring Spring
Exploring Autumn
Science Mini-Mysteries
Power Up
The Kids' Earth Handbook

EXPLORING AUTUMN

by Sandra Markle

*A Season of Science
Activities, Puzzlers,
and Games*

Atheneum   1991   New York

Maxwell Macmillan Canada
Toronto

Maxwell Macmillan International

New York   Oxford   Singapore   Sydney

For Leanna Landsmann
*Thanks for opening
so many doors for me*

LIBRARY OF CONGRESS CATALOGING-IN-PUBLICATION DATA
Markle, Sandra.
Exploring autumn: a season of science activities, puzzlers, and
games / by Sandra Markle.—1st ed.
p.   cm.
Includes index.
Summary: A collection of facts, games, riddles, and other
activities, related to the autumn season.
ISBN 0-889-31620-8
1. Autumn—Juvenile literature.   2. Nature study—Juvenile
literature.   3. Amusements—Juvenile literature.   [1. Autumn.
2. Nature study.   3. Amusements.]   I. Title.
QH81.M2654   1991
574.5'43—dc20   90-24209
Atheneum
Macmillan Publishing Company
866 Third Avenue
New York, NY 10022

Maxwell Macmillan Canada, Inc.
1200 Eglinton Avenue East
Suite 200
Don Mills, Ontario M3C 3N1
First edition

Macmillan Publishing Company is
part of the Maxwell Communication Group
of Companies.

Printed in the United States of America

1 2 3 4 5 6 7 8 9 10

CONTENTS

Is It Autumn Yet?   vii

1. A SEASON OF CHANGES   1
   Timely Changes · Making Days Longer · When Fall Lost Ten Days · Pretty Frosty · Why Do Leaves Change Color? · Unbe-LEAF-able Action · Sealed for the Winter · New Uses for Old Leaves · Make a Colorful Leaf Collage · Print Your Own Note Cards · Indian Summer · Fall Wildflowers · Bouncing Bet · Goldenrod · Joe-Pye Weed · Closed Gentian · Aster · Pokeweed · A Star Drama

2. HARVEST TIME   25
   Autumn's Bounty · Apples · In the Sauce · Carve an Apple Head · Johnny Appleseed · Corn (Maize) · Make a Cornhusk Doll · Goober Peas · Make Your Own Peanut Butter · Cotton · Make a Bird Shooter · Bringing in the Crops · Going to Seed · Maple Trees · Dandelions · Tumbleweeks · Cattails · Sticktights · Mistletoe · Seed Poppers · Peek inside a Seed · Go on a Seed Hunt · Seedy Art · Thanksgiving around the World · The Truth about the Pilgrims · Answers to The Truth about the Pilgrims · Moving to the New World · The Amazing Adventures of Squanto · Bounce the Berry · The National Turkey

3. HAPPY HALLOWEEN   65
   Celebrating Samhain · Mixing Customs · Trick-or-Treating · Who Is That Masked Person—Really? · Make a Monster of Yourself · Jack-o'-Lanterns · Carve a Bogie · Grow Your Own Giant Jack-o'-Lanterns · Pumpkin Faces · Seedy Treat · Witches and Wizards · The Mean, the Bad, and the Nasty · Scorpions · Lionfish · Great White Sharks · Black Widow Spiders · Fire Ants · African Killer Bees · Cobras ·

Mosquitoes · Wolverines · *The Truth about Vampires* · *Real Dragons* · *Eyes That Glow in the Dark* · *Boning Up on Bones* · *Super Big, Super Old Bones* · *It's Party Time* · *Snap an Apple* · *Grab Some Guts* · *Bend a Bone* · *Make Ghostly Noises* · *Stir Up a Witch's Brew* · *Cause a Spooky Arm Lift*

4. MORE SEASONAL ACTION   106
Rosh Hashanah · *Columbus Day* · *Sail Your Own* Niña, Pinta, *and* Santa María · *Was There Someone Before Columbus?* · *Fall Festival of Lights* · *Electing a U.S. President* · *A Little Party History* · *Presidential Stumpers* · *Presidents of the United States* · *It Can't Be Right!* · *Answers to Presidential Stumpers* · *A Tropical Terror*

5. ANIMALS IN AUTUMN   129
A Fall Song · *Dressed for Success* · *Pretty Foxy* · *The Truth about Ants in Autumn* · *On the Ant Trail* · *Autumn Travelers* · *Canada Geese* · *Other Flocks to Watch For* · *Where Are They Going?* · *Bison* · *Eels* · *Traveling Fish* · *New Fall Coats* · *Fall's Feast* · *Storing It Away* · *Getting Their Houses Ready for Winter* · *Winter Sleepers*

THE END (FOR THIS YEAR)   149
INDEX   150

IS IT AUTUMN YET?

IS IT autumn yet? Do you hear loud chirping insect songs you hadn't noticed before? Have you spotted a flock of birds overhead looking like a dark, living cloud, winging determinedly south? Do some trees show hints of brilliant colors—yellows, oranges, and rusty hues—among their usual green?

Autumn floats down on you and piles up around your feet. It's fields of ripe wheat being pushed into golden swells by the wind, fat orange pumpkins on shriveled vines, bees rushing to find the last flowers, and squirrels burying nuts in the dirt. Autumn is crisp apples that fill your mouth with sweet juice. It's the city pool closing and school opening.

This is the season when your toes get pinched by new shoes, when you're surprised one morning to see the grass glistening white with the first frost, and when you watch football being played to the music of marching bands. Autumn is bright, busy, splashed with out-of-the-ordinary colors, and delicious.

Is it autumn yet? Almost? Then this book is for you.

It has investigations to help you discover the way the world changes in autumn and instructions for building things to enjoy during this season. There are wildflowers to look for and a myth about the constellations you can see on a fall night. You'll find out why one year autumn was ten days shorter than normal, learn the history of Halloween, and discover some real monsters. You can create pressed-leaf art, make cornhusk dolls, and whip up peanut butter. There are lots of activities perfect for throwing a spooky Halloween party, directions for building boats for a Columbus Day race, and investigations that will keep you exploring all autumn long. There are games to play, riddles to laugh at, quizzes to challenge you, and lots of facts to amaze you.

This book is guaranteed to bring out that secret desire to become an explorer that lurks inside you.

Is it autumn yet? Get ready. Autumn is too intriguing to miss.

1.
A SEASON
OF CHANGES

Timely Changes

AUTUMN OFFICIALLY begins on September 23 with the autumnal equinox, the day when the number of hours of daylight equals the number of hours of darkness. It officially ends on December 21, the shortest day of the year. These two key days are created by a combination of the earth's tilt and its movement orbiting around the sun.

As you can see in the diagram below, the earth doesn't travel through space with the North Pole pointed straight up. The earth is tilted. So for part of its yearlong trip around the sun—spring and summer—the North Pole is aimed more and more directly at the sun. Then for the remainder of the year—fall and winter—the moving earth directs its North Pole farther and farther away from the sun. Autumn, like spring, is a season of transition between the two extremes—having the northern hemisphere aimed most directly at the sun and having it pointed most completely away from the sun.

Wonder why the earth's orbit and tilt make so much difference in the climate? Try sitting directly under a lighted table lamp with a sheet of paper on your lap. Notice how bright the light is that strikes the paper. Sit there for five minutes. You should also notice a feeling of warmth. Now, move about six feet away from the light. Finally, move about twelve feet away. With each move, the light striking your paper becomes dimmer. There is also little if any noticeable warmth from the light the farther away from it you are.

The region at the earth's equator receives about the same amount of sunlight year round. In the northern and southern hemispheres, though, there are seasonal changes because of the number of hours that this part of the earth receives direct sunlight.

Sunlight doesn't warm the air very much as it passes through, however. Instead, sunlight is absorbed by rocks and soil and water and even buildings on the surface. Then these features warm up and radiate heat into the air. In autumn, less direct sunlight and shorter days mean less time for exposure to sunlight and create cooler weather.

Earth orbiting Sun

Making Days Longer

SINCE THE beginning of time, nature controlled when it was daylight and dark. People simply adjusted their schedules to follow this natural clock, rising with the sun and going to bed when it got dark. Later, as artificial methods for lighting were developed, people were able to start work before sunrise and keep on working long past sunset. So for factories, running on a set schedule became more important than working during daylight hours.

Then, in 1907, William Willet, an Englishman, published a

pamphlet called "Waste of Daylight," suggesting that daylight saving time be adopted. He saw this as a way to once more take advantage of daylight as a source of light for workers. The idea didn't catch on until Germany did it during World War I, in an effort to conserve the fuel needed to produce electricity. Shortly after that, Great Britain and much of western Europe tried what was called "summer time" as a way to conserve energy. The United States and portions of Canada also adopted daylight saving time as a wartime measure in 1917. But when World War I was over, so was this time-saving idea.

Daylight saving time wasn't observed again until 1942, when it was reinstated during World War II to conserve fuel. Today, daylight saving time is observed mainly as a way to allow people more daylight hours to enjoy themselves outdoors after work.

In the United States, daylight saving time officially begins on the first Sunday in April and ends on the last Sunday in October. To remember which way to set your clock, just think of this saying: "Fall back, spring forward." This means that you set your clock back an hour in the fall and ahead an hour in the spring.

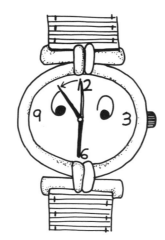

Daylight Saving Time

When Fall Lost Ten Days

A CALENDAR year marks the length of time that it takes the earth to make one trip around the sun. However, the earth actually takes a little longer to complete its orbit than 365 days. In fact, it actually takes the earth 365 days, five hours, forty-eight minutes, and forty-six seconds. When the calendar was first established in ancient times, the people just worked with 365 days because no one thought the extra little bit of time would make any difference. But it did. So Julius Caesar, ruler of ancient Rome, declared the calendar year to officially be 365¼ days long. And he added Leap Day, an extra day every fourth year. So every fourth year February has twenty-nine days instead of only twenty-eight.

For a number of centuries, the Leap Year tradition seemed to keep the calendar and the earth's travels synchronized. However, creating Leap Day still didn't quite make things equal. The earth actually takes eleven minutes and fourteen seconds less than 365¼ days to completely orbit the sun every year. So once again after a number of centuries, the calendar and normal seasonal events no longer matched. By the late 1500s, the autumnal equinox, for example, was observed to occur ten whole days before it was expected according to the calendar.

This was too great a discrepancy to live with any longer. Pope Gregory XIII declared that the calendar had to be changed once again. And it was decided that this could best be accomplished by changing the way Leap Day was handled. Following the new approach, there would be a Leap Day every fourth year except in a year that could be divided by 100 but not by 400. This meant that the years 1700, 1800, and 1900 were not Leap Years, but 2000 will be Leap Year. This calendar manipulation saves three days every 400

Changing Calendar

years. Finally, to bring the calendar back on track, Pope Gregory declared that the day after October 4, 1582, was officially October 15, 1582, making that autumn ten days shorter than normal.

Not every country was willing to correct its calendar in 1582, however. England waited to fix up its calendar until 1752. By that time, the dates were another whole day off and people had to lose eleven days. This led to riots as workers and landlords felt they were being cheated out of wages and rent. China didn't correct its calendar until the beginning of the twentieth century. Russia and Greece didn't make the switch until after World War I.

Unfortunately, Pope Gregory's correction still didn't make the calendar perfect. The calendar year is still longer than the earth's actual orbiting time. So in about 10,000 years the naturally occurring events will seem to occur too early once again—but only by about two days this time.

Quack!

What do you get when you cross an owl with a duck?
A wise quacker

Pretty Frosty

IN PARTS of the world where there are definite seasons, autumn is time for a change in the weather. And one of the most dramatic changes is the first frost. Frost is a coating of ice crystals that forms on everything from plants to windowpanes. It occurs when the amount of water vapor or moisture in the air is high; there is little wind; and the temperature at ground level drops below 32 degrees Fahrenheit—the freezing temperature for water. Frost is more likely to occur on clear nights than on cloudy nights because cloud cover helps slow down the loss of heat being radiated away from the earth's surface. Frost may be little spikelike columns. Or it may be flat snowflakelike crystals.

You don't have to wait for nature to observe frost, though. You can simulate the weather conditions that create frost and produce some to look at up close. To do this, you'll need a carton or plastic bucket of ice cream. Take it out of the freezer section of the refrigerator and place it on the table. Wait a couple of minutes and then take a close look at the outside of the container. It will be coated with frost. What does the frost look like? Scrape some off with your fingernail. What does it feel like?

The frost formed because water vapor in the air came in contact with the cold container. In nature, water vapor in the air is chilled by cold air close to the ground. If the water vapor is not chilled to the freezing point, droplets of water called dew form on the container instead of frost. When the air is freezing cold, the water vapor changes directly from a gas to solid ice crystals.

A coating of frost can be beautiful, transforming the world into a dazzling crystal wonderland on a cold, sunny fall morning. Frost damages delicate plant tissues, though, by causing the fluid inside plant cells to freeze and expand. Then when the sun comes out and the plant tissues begin to warm up again, the cells burst. A heavy frost causes one of the most noticeable changes in autumn by killing plants and bringing the growing season to an end. Only evergreens, such as pines and firs, survive. Their leaves have a waxy coating that protects them from frost damage.

Why Do Leaves Change Color?

DECIDUOUS TREES, trees for which the coming winter will be a season of rest, reveal one of the most obvious signs that summer is past and autumn has begun. Their leaves change color and eventually drop off. It's for this very reason that autumn is sometimes called "fall."

The colorful change made by deciduous trees happens because food production slows and finally stops. The tree's leaves are its food factory. And to produce food the leaf's cells must contain chlorophyll.

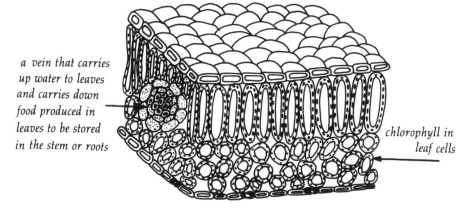

Inside a leaf

a vein that carries up water to leaves and carries down food produced in leaves to be stored in the stem or roots

chlorophyll in leaf cells

Chlorophyll is a green pigment that helps the cells capture the sun's energy and use it in combination with water and carbon dioxide gas from the air to produce sugars, the tree's food supply. During this food production process, called photosynthesis, some of the chlorophyll is constantly being broken down. But during the growing season, more chlorophyll is manufactured to replace what is lost.

There is another group of coloring pigments present in the leaves called carotenes. These are yellow, brown, and shades of orange. As long as there is chlorophyll present, though, the carotene colors are hidden by the bright green. In autumn, as the days grown shorter, food production slows. Chlorophyll production also slows, so that gradually the supply dwindles. Then the green mask fades, revealing the rich shades produced by the carotene pigments.

Yellow is the most common color of autumn leaves. If you live where the leaves change color, count for yourself how many different kinds of trees have leaves that are a shade of yellow. You're sure to find them in yellow poplars, aspens, sycamore, and sassafras trees.

Some of the most beautifully colored fall leaves, however, are shades of red. The pigments that paint these leaves are called anthocyanins. They develop when the sugar produced in the leaves is trapped there. Normally, special tubes form pipelines, carrying water from the tree to the leaves and carrying the sugar away. When chlorophyll production stops, a layer of corky cells develops across the point where the leaf joins the branch, sealing it off. Water can no longer reach the leaf and any sugar that is produced by the remaining chlorophyll is trapped. As the trapped sugar breaks down, red anthocyanin pigments are produced. There is more trapped sugar to produce brilliant reds when there is a combination of bright sunny days and cool nights.

Unbe-LEAF-able Action

IMPATIENT TO see the trees change color and shed their leaves? Then don't wait another minute to follow the steps below and make this fall flip book.

1. First, you'll need five sheets of plain white typing paper. Fold each sheet into fourths and cut the sections apart, creating twenty mini-pages.

2. Next, draw the picture of a tree in the very center of one of the mini-pages. Show it covered with green leaves.

3. Place a second page over the first. Trace the outline of the tree, but this time color it, showing just a hint of autumn yellow, orange, or red.

4. Repeat this process with the next page, giving the tree a little more color.

5. By the time you have retraced the tree on the eighth page, show it in full color. Then on pages nine through nineteen show the tree with leaves floating down, an increasing number of bare branches visible, and leaves piling up at the base of the trunk.

6. Show a bare tree with a pile of leaves at its base on the last page.

7. Finally, stack the mini-pages in order from the green tree through the bare tree. And staple this along the left-hand edge—near the top, near the bottom, and in the middle.

Now, anytime you want to see the tree change into its autumn foliage and shed its leaves, just flip rapidly through the book from front to back.

Sealed for the Winter

WHEN AUTUMN leaves are lying on the ground, take a close look at a tree branch. You'll see round, oval, and even horseshoe-shaped scars where the leaves were attached. Look at one scar with a magnifying glass and you'll see clusters of tiny dots. These are the sealed ends of the tubes that were connected to the leaf's veins, carrying water up from the roots and sugar down from the leaves to be stored in the trunk or the roots. Did you notice the small bump just above the leaf scar on the branch? This is a bud. Inside, protected against winter's harsh weather, is the tiny folded leaf that will grow and produce food for the tree next spring and summer.

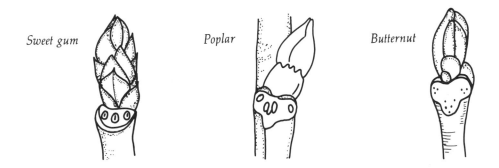

Sweet gum   *Poplar*   *Butternut*

New Uses for Old Leaves

RECYCLING IS nothing new in nature. Fallen leaves provide shelter and food for the larvae, or young, of beetles and other insects. Rotting leaves also supply food for mushrooms and other fungi because these don't produce chlorophyll. This means they can't manufacture their own food. As the leaves further decay, they help make the soil more fertile, supplying the minerals needed by other growing plants.

Leaves that fall into streams are recycled too. Stonefly larvae, for example, shred the leaves, gobbling down tiny particles. Because they're sloppy eaters, though, many tiny leaf bits float away, becoming food for midges, blackflies, and other stream insects. All of these, in turn, become dinner for frogs and fish. And so the food chain goes, starting with the leaves the trees couldn't use any longer.

*How does a farmer get his hogs
to market?*
In a pig-up truck.

Make a Colorful Leaf Collage

SOME LEAVES are such beautiful shades of red, yellow, orange, or rust that they look like works of art. So why not use them to create something special? Start by collecting the most beautiful leaves you can find. These don't always have to be undamaged leaves. Fall leaves with a few insect bites or a wind-tattered corner are sometimes the most interesting.

Next, flatten the leaves by placing them between sections of newspaper and then stacking heavy books on top. Wait overnight. Then lay out a sheet of clear contact paper with the sticky side up. Arrange the leaves in a pattern on the center of this sheet. Cover with a second sheet of clear contact paper—sticky side down—sealing the leaves inside. Press close to the edges of the leaves with your fingertips.

Finally, cut the plastic into a geometric shape, such as a big circle or octagon. Be careful not to cut through any of the leaves. Punch a hole in the top of the plastic with a hole punch and add a ribbon loop to hang up your collage. This pressed-leaf art is especially pretty hung in a window where light can shine through the colored leaves.

Print Your Own Note Cards

YOU CAN use some of nature's artistry to create special cards you can use to write to your friends. First, you'll need to collect more fallen leaves. This time choose small leaves with interesting shapes. As you did before, place these leaves between sections of newspaper and press under heavy books overnight.

You'll also need water-based printer's ink or acrylic paint (available at craft and hobby stores), a brush, rubber gloves (the kind used for washing dishes or doing painting projects), an old shirt or a plastic garbage bag with head- and arm-holes cut in it to protect your clothes, construction paper, and a garbage can with a plastic liner. Cover your work area with newspaper. Next, fold the construction paper sheets in half horizontally. Cut along this creased line. Then fold each new piece in half again horizontally.

When you're ready to print, put on your cover-up and gloves. Lay one of the leaves down on the newspaper. If the veins show more prominently on one side, place that side up. The veins will add interesting texture to your print.

Next, brush-paint all over the leaf's surface. Then carefully move the leaf to a clean spot on the newspaper and lay your folded construction paper—front down—on top of it. With your hand, press the leaf through the paper from the stem end up.

You may want to make several prints of a single leaf on one note card to make a design. Or you may want to make a single leaf print on each of several different note cards. You could also combine prints of several different leaves on one note card. Be creative!

You'll be able to make several leaf prints from one coating of ink or paint. Each print, though, will be a little lighter than the one before. When you've finished with a leaf, throw it into the garbage can.

After the leaf prints have dried completely, the note cards are ready for you to use. Or you may want to put together a selection of your leaf-print note cards and tie the pack with a ribbon. This would make a great gift!

Indian Summer

THIS TERM has come to mean any period of warm, sunny weather following a hard frost. The Europeans who moved to North America and settled in regions that had definite seasons coined this expression. They discovered that the Native Americans or Indians they encountered in their new homeland sometimes played tricks on them. They reasoned that these summer-warm fall days were a similar trick being played on them by nature because the warm weather couldn't be counted on to last.

Fall Wildflowers

AUTUMN DOESN'T bring an end to flowering plants until after the first killing frost, but there is a change in the kinds of plants that you'll see blooming. A wildflower is any flower that grows and blooms untended in woods and meadows, along streams and roads, and even in vacant city lots. In places where winters bring a long period of rest for plants, fall wildflowers are all the more special because they're the last blooms of the year.

Here are some wildflowers you can hunt for in the fall. To see what they really look like, place a sheet of tracing paper over the page, trace the flower, and then color it according to the directions.

Start a collection of drawings or photos of the wildflowers you find. Use books to help you learn the names of these fall flowers. And be sure to include information on where you discovered them. Leave the real plants growing, though, so others can enjoy them and so you can find them again next fall.

Bouncing Bet

THIS PLANT is sometimes called the soapwort because a soapy lather can be made by crushing its leaves in water. In pioneer days, Bouncing Bet was used by women to shampoo their hair and to wash fine wools and linens.

The flat-looking flowers, which bloom from July through September, have a spicy smell that is strongest at night. The plants are often pollinated by night-flying moths. Bouncing Bet was introduced to this country from Europe and has spread throughout the United States. It thrives in places where the land has been cleared. Its network of spreading underground stems help anchor the bare soil.

The flowers are pink. The one-to-two-foot-high stalks and leaves are bright green.

Goldenrod

THERE ARE about a hundred different varieties of goldenrods growing throughout Canada and the United States, so in the late summer and fall, it's one of the most common wildflowers. In fact, it's the state flower of Alabama, Kentucky, and Nebraska.

Growing up to four feet tall and topped with spikes or clusters of tiny flowers, the goldenrod is easy to spot and to identify. Unfortunately, it has gained a bad reputation, being blamed for many people's hay-fever problems. In truth, the goldenrod's heavy pollen is rarely carried very far by the wind. Usually, it's the light pollen of the ragweed plants, which also bloom in the fall, that causes most sneezes and stuffy noses.

While the clusters of flowers are arranged on the stem differently in different species, they're all yellow except for silverrod. It has white flowers. The leaves are green and the stem is greenish brown.

Joe-Pye Weed

TO SPOT these flowers, look up. The blooms sit atop straight stems that stretch up to fifteen feet high. The Joe-Pye weed blooms from July through September in the moist soils of thick woods and along shaded roadsides in the eastern half of the United States and

Canada. If you look closely, you'll see that the blooms are actually made up of many small flower heads. Look still closer and you'll discover that these smaller flowers are in turn made up of many tiny flowers.

Joe-Pye weed is supposedly named after an Indian medicine man who helped the early colonists in Massachusetts. According to legend, Joe Pye cured a number of different illnesses by preparing medicine from these giant wildflowers.

The flowers range from pinkish white to pale purple. The leaves are dark green and the stems are purplish green.

Closed Gentian

WHEN YOU find this plant, you'll have to decide what to call it. In different places, it's called closed gentian, bottle gentian, barrel gentian, and blind gentian. All of these names refer to the fact that the flowers resemble little barrels or bottles. These blooms develop

in clusters encircling the stem near the top of straight, one-to-two-foot-tall plants. Preferring moist ground, the closed gentian is found throughout eastern North America from Canada to Georgia. Its flowers are pollinated by bumblebees who must push inside the bloom to gather pollen.

The blooms are bright blue. The leaves are bright green and the stem and central leaf vein are brownish green. Notice that the lower leaves are paired on opposite sides of the stem. The upper leaves, like the blooms, are whorled, meaning that they encircle the stem.

Aster

THERE ARE more than two hundred species of asters growing in North America. Many of these grow in open fields with goldenrod, creating a colorful autumn display. The leaves are arranged alternately on the stem and the flowers are clustered in a bouquet at the top. The blooms are actually flower heads made up of yellow disk flowers in the middle and colored ray flowers that are often mistaken for petals.

This is the New England aster. It sometimes grows to be over five feet tall. Its flowers are deep purple. Its stout stem and leaves are dark green.

Pokeweed

YOU'LL FIND this plant mainly in the east from New England to Florida and west to Texas and north to Minnesota. It's the drooping clusters of purplish black berries that are eye-catching. Despite how pretty they are, the pokeberries are poisonous, so don't eat any. Some people collect and eat this plant's new green shoots when they poke through the ground, however. And the early colonists used pokeberry juice to dye cloth.

The pokeweed is a tall plant, growing up to ten feet high. It prefers open areas that have been recently cleared, such as unplanted fields and roadsides. Ripening fruit and even ripe fruit are often on the plant while it's still blooming.

The small flowers are white. The berries are very dark purplish black. The stems are red and the leaves are bright green.

A Star Drama

THE STARS you can see in the nighttime sky also change in autumn. Many of the constellations during this period run into each other or overlap, so the patterns aren't as clear as during the other seasons. There also aren't as many dramatically bright stars. However, all the characters of a very exciting legend appear together.

According to the story, Queen Cassiopeia and King Cepheus had a beautiful young daughter, Andromeda, of whom they were extremely proud. In fact, the queen boasted that Andromeda was even more beautiful than the sea nymphs.

Bragging is never good, and this particular boast was especially bad because it offended the sea nymphs. Angry and upset, they demanded that Nereus, the sea god, do something to make Cassiopeia sorry for her remarks. So Nereus sent a terrible serpent who began devouring the people in great numbers. No one in King Cepheus' kingdom dared go out fishing or even to the shore for fear of being caught and eaten.

The king sent his best soldiers to kill the serpent, but they all failed. Finally, King Cepheus learned that the only way to get rid of this sea beast was to feed him one princess—Andromeda. The king and queen were sick with grief, but they had no choice. Their whole kingdom was at risk if they didn't obey. So poor, beautiful Andromeda was chained to a rock by the sea to await her fate.

However, just as the serpent rose from the waves to swallow the princess, a young, handsome adventurer named Perseus, who had just killed the evil Medusa, arrived on winged shoes. Seeing what was about to happen, Perseus rushed to Andromeda's rescue. After he killed the serpent, he returned the princess to her parents and asked for her hand in marriage. The king and queen were thankful their daughter had been saved and were glad to grant Perseus' wish.

The constellations for all the characters in this story can be found close together in the autumn sky. To spot them first find Polaris, the North Star. The Big Dipper will appear on one side of Polaris. Directly opposite it, you'll see what looks like a *W* or an *M*, depending on your point of view. That's Cassiopeia, the queen. The group of stars to the left of Cassiopeia form Perseus. Those to the south form Andromeda. She can be recognized by the line of bright stars—one in her head, one for her belt, and one on her feet. Cepheus, the king, is formed by the stars to Cassiopeia's right.

Perseus

Andromeda

Feeling hungry? There's plenty to eat in autumn. You'll find out all about the harvest and discover some terrific seasonal activities in the next chapter.

2.
HARVEST
TIME

Autumn's Bounty

A TRADITIONAL autumn symbol is the cornucopia or horn overflowing with fruits, vegetables, nuts, and even fall flowers. The story behind this harvest symbol comes from ancient Greece. According to legend, when the god Zeus was an infant he was tended by a nymph named Amalthea, who raised him on goat's milk. Later, the grateful young god broke off one of the goat's horns and gave it to his foster mother filled with fruit and flowers. With this, the horn became a magic horn, and Amalthea had only to wish for something to have the horn supply it. This horn of plenty seems a fitting symbol for a season when so many crops reach maturity. Here are just a few examples. See how many more you can think of that are harvested in the fall.

Apples

ACCORDING TO the familiar saying, eating one of these a day will keep you healthy. Apples are definitely nourishing as well as tasty. This fruit contains a natural sugar that makes it a great snack food because it supplies the body with a quick energy source while being low in calories—an average apple contains only about eighty calories. Apples are also low in sodium, high in fiber, and contain no cholesterol—all important for maintaining a healthy body. As a bonus, the crisp juicy texture of the apple helps to massage gums and clean teeth.

Although there are thousands of different kinds of apples, only a dozen of the most popular are regularly grown and harvested for

Cortland
green around stem, red overall,
with a hint of yellow at base
slightly tart and tender, snow-
white flesh

Golden Delicious
greenish yellow
sweet and juicy

Red Delicious
red, sweet, tender, juicy

McIntosh
red above and green on bottom
tart and juicy

market: Red Delicious, Golden Delicious, McIntosh, Rome Beauty, York, Jonathan, Granny Smith, Stayman Winesap, Cortland, Northern Spy, and Gravenstein. Of these, Red Delicious are especially popular for eating fresh because of their color and crunch. Tarter varieties, such as Granny Smith, Cortland, and York, are preferred for baking.

Different kinds of apples are different colors, shapes, and sizes. Their flesh is also different colors and textures and these vary in how sweet they taste. Compare some of the most popular varieties for yourself. Try to find at least four different types of apples. Wash your test samples, then take a bite of each in turn. Rinse your mouth out with water and wait at least one minute between each test.

As you chew, rate each apple on a scale of 1 (least) to 4 (most) for sweetness. It's okay to have more than one apple receive the same score. Take another bite and rate the apples on texture, with 1 being the softest and 4 being the firmest. Finally, finish eating the apple you gave the highest combined score. Wrap the other apples in clear wrap and store in the refrigerator for later.

It's estimated that the average person in the United States consumes about fifty apples a year. So while you're making this comparison test, you'll be on your way to eating your fair share of this year's crop.

RIDDLE

What kind of fruit do ghosts like?
Booberries.

In the Sauce

A POPULAR way to store apples for later is to turn them into applesauce. Have an adult partner work with you to cook some up following this recipe.

You'll need: 10 tart apples, 1 cup apple cider, 1 cup water, ¾ cup brown sugar, 2 teaspoons cinnamon, ½ teaspoon vanilla, ½ teaspoon salt, a knife, a cutting board, a saucepan, a spoon, a measuring cup, and measuring spoons.

First, peel, core, and dice the apples. Put the diced apples in a saucepan and pour on the cider and water. Cook over very low heat until the apples are soft. Stir until a smooth sauce is formed. Then add the spices, stir again, and cool before eating.

Carve an Apple Head

APPLES ARE sometimes carved and allowed to shrink and dry to make heads for dolls. Even if you don't want to make a doll, you can still have fun carving an apple. It's also interesting to watch the apple face you create "age" as the fruit dries and shrinks. You'll need the largest firm apple you can find, a cutting board, a peeler, a knife, a bowl, measuring spoons, water, and salt.

First, peel the apple. You may want to leave some peel on top for hair. Next, plan what you want the face to look like. A spooky old witch's face is a good choice. Next, working on the cutting board, carve away parts of the apple to create eye sockets, cheeks, a nose, mouth, and ears.

When you're finished, pour one quart (4 cups) of water into the bowl and stir in a teaspoon of salt. Place the carved apple in the water for two hours. This will soften the fruit's flesh. Now, use your fingers and the eraser end of a pencil to finish molding and shaping your apple head. You may want to push raisins into the eye sockets for eyes or poke in kernels of popcorn for teeth.

Set your completed apple head on a plate. To speed up the drying process, place the apple head in a sunny spot. Check daily. How does the color of the apple head change as it dries? What other ways does the face change?

Notice that the dried apple isn't moldy. One way that people used to preserve food for use during the winter was to dry it. The lower moisture content discourages bacteria and mold growth.

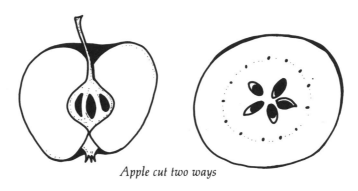

Apple cut two ways

Johnny Appleseed

IT HAS been said that many of the apple orchards in Ohio, Illinois, Iowa, and Indiana were originally planted by John Chapman, better known as Johnny Appleseed. This folk hero of the late 1700s supposedly spent forty years planting apple seeds that he'd collected from cider mills as he traveled back and forth between the settled farmlands of the east and the frontier. And to further spread his beloved apple trees, Johnny passed out seeds and young seedlings to new settlers and to pioneers heading west.

While Johnny Appleseed's efforts are still appreciated and remembered, apple trees are rarely grown from seeds today. It takes several years for trees to grow big enough to begin to bear fruit, and there's no way to be sure that trees grown from seed will produce desirable fruit. So in order to be certain of the variety, apple trees are grown by *grafting*—inserting a twig or bud from a tree that is known to bear an abundant crop of terrific-tasting apples into the stem of a strong young sapling. Then any of the sapling's own branches are pruned away. By the time the tree starts to bear, only branches that grew from the graft will be producing fruit.

Corn (Maize)

CORN IS a plant that is native to the Americas. In fact, it was such an important food crop that the ancient Aztecs, Mayas, Incas, and many other Native American peoples considered corn a god or a gift from the gods. Ceremonies with dances and prayers were performed to encourage the gods to help the seeds sprout and the young plants to grow. Special harvest festivals were held to say "thank you" for a bountiful crop.

Corn was a term used in Europe to refer to any kind of cereal grain, such as wheat, oats, or barley. The kind of corn that is native

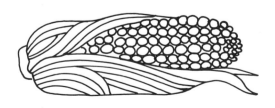

to the Americas is maize. Like the other grains, maize is related to grass. However, unlike these other plants, maize can't grow successfully without man's help because it's unable to spread its own seeds.

Each kernel of corn on a cob is a seed. If a cob fell to the ground, many of the seeds would sprout—so many that there wouldn't be room for any of the young plants to grow. People must remove the seeds from the cob and plant them where they will have plenty of growing space. Native Americans learned to plant a few kernels of corn in a small hill of dirt. Today, farmers use machines to dig shallow trenches in the soil and drop in seeds that are just the right distance apart.

There are a number of different kinds of corn: popcorn, sweet corn, flour corn, flint corn, and dent corn. Indian corn looked very different from the corn that's generally eaten today. For one thing, it was different colors. Some of the kernels were red, blue, and black, as well as yellow and white. In the southwest, blue corn is still considered to have the best flavor.

To store corn, the husks or protective outer leaves must be stripped off so it can be dried. Husking corn was a hard, time-consuming job, so farmers held husking bees or parties, and people from surrounding farms came to share the work. This often became the big social event of the year, with plenty of music and lots of refreshments for the workers. Machines have made husking corn a lot easier but a lot less fun.

Besides being a valuable source of vitamins and protein, a nutrient needed by the body to grow and repair itself, corn has many other uses. It's used as animal feed. Corn oil is processed to produce margarine, cooking oil, and soap. Corn starch is used in manufacturing glue, paper, powders, and more. Corn sugar is used to make corn syrup.

Make a Cornhusk Doll

(Thanks to Diane Mickleson of Samuell Farm, a division of Dallas Parks and Recreation, Dallas, Texas, for sharing these instructions.)

TO MAKE this harvesttime doll, you'll need ten dried cornhusks, one yard of yarn, six 4-inch-long pieces of yarn or a bundle of dried corn silk for hair, scissors, a large paper clip, a large mixing bowl, and warm tap water.

You can dry the cornhusks yourself. Just save the ones you pull off ears of corn on the cob and let them dry in the sun or spread out on newspapers indoors. If you dry them indoors, you'll need to change the paper under the husks daily. Once completely dried, the husks will be a light brown color and can be stored indefinitely if kept dry.

Or you can purchase dried cornhusks. They're inexpensive and may be available in your local grocery store in the specialty-foods area because the husks are used to prepare tamales. If not, write to Ralph Foods, Box 125, Edroy, Texas 78352 (or call 1-800-423-6090, or in Texas 1-800-221-5135) for information on purchasing dried cornhusks through the mail.

To make a cornhusk doll, you first need to soak nine unbroken cornhusks in a bowlful of warm tap water for about ten minutes or until they are soft. If you want to color some of the cornhusks, such as the ones that you'll use for the doll's dress, soak these overnight in water that has been colored with food coloring. Then follow these steps:

1. To form the hair, arrange the yarn pieces or corn silk to form a neat bundle

and tie in the middle with a short piece of yarn. Tie a knot and trim off the ends close to the bundle.

2.   Select one narrow cornhusk to make the stuffing for inside the doll's head. Fold in the edges on either side. Next fold over the pointed end. Then roll up the husk to form a wad.

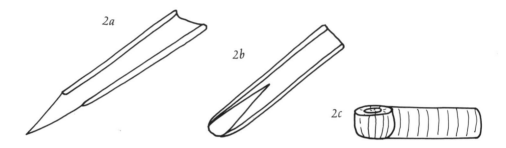

2a

2b

2c

3.   Pick another narrow cornhusk for the face. Feel the husk and notice that one side is ridged while the other is smooth. Place the stuffing on the middle of the ridged side, lay the hair directly above it, and fold over the husk. Tie a piece of yarn tightly around the "neck."

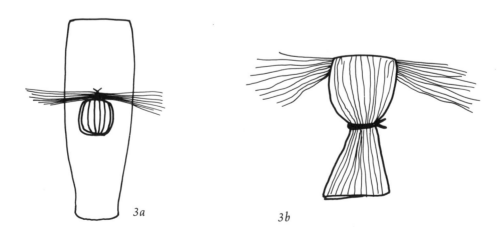

3a

3b

4. Next, choose a fairly wide husk for the arms. Fold this in half, and then roll it into a tube. Tie pieces of yarn about three-fourths of an inch in from each end at what would be the doll's wrist to hold this tube together.

5. Slide the arms between the flaps below the head. And tie with yarn directly below the arms to hold them tightly in place.

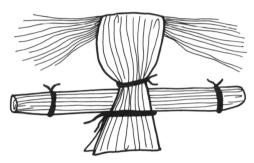

6. The body of the doll is actually a full dress. Make this by placing one full husk over the front of the doll, covering the yarn tied under the arms. Cover the back with a second and third husk. Then finish with a final husk over the front. You may need someone to tie a piece of yarn around the doll's waist

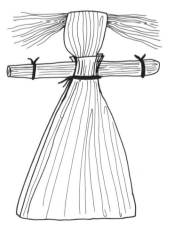

while you hold the husks in place. Trim off the tops of the husks used to form the dress so they're even with the arms. Also trim the bottom so the hem of the skirt is even. This will allow the doll to stand.

7. To finish the doll's dress, you'll need two narrow husks. Fold each in half. Then crisscross the folded husks across the top of the doll as shown—folded edge toward the arms. Tie another piece of yarn around the doll's waist to hold this shirt in place. You may want to finish this tie in a bow at the doll's back.

8. Trim off any excess ends of yarn close to the doll's body. Fold the final husk in half and wrap it around the doll's skirt, paper-clipping the ends together. This will prevent the husks from spreading and curling as they dry. Let the doll dry completely—about twenty-four hours—and remove the husk holding the skirt. Then you may want to use fine-tipped paint pens (available at craft stores) to add a face. You could also paint flowers on the doll's dress.

Goober Peas

NEVER HEARD of this crop? Sure you have. Goober peas is another name for peanuts. In a way it's a better name because peanuts aren't nuts at all. They're related to peas and beans. The peanuts or seeds develop inside pods underground.

Peanuts are believed to have originated in South America. The Spanish conquistadores were introduced to this food by the Incas of Peru and took them home to Spain, where they became an important crop. Peanuts became a favorite food in Africa too when the Spanish and Portuguese traded them for spices and ivory. And then, when blacks were brought from Africa to be slaves in North America, peanuts came along. Despite being nourishing, they didn't

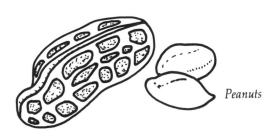

Peanuts

gain favor in the United States, though, until the Civil War. Soldiers discovered that peanuts were an easy-to-prepare, easy-to-carry, tasty, quick energy food.

The person who really made the peanut a success, though, was Dr. George Washington Carver. When poor soil and insect pests made it impossible for southern farmers to make a profit raising cotton, Dr. Carver suggested they plant peanuts. And through his experiments, he discovered over three hundred uses for the peanut to help create new markets for this crop. These are just a few of the many products produced from peanuts—both the nut meat and the plant: peanut butter, mayonnaise, margarine, cheese, shaving cream, ink, plastics, cosmetics, shampoo, fertilizer, and shoe polish.

Make Your Own Peanut Butter

PEANUT BUTTER was first developed by a physician in St. Louis who wanted to find an easy-to-eat, nutritious food for his elderly patients. Now it's a popular food for all ages. To make your own, you'll need a blender, 1 cup of freshly roasted peanuts (salted or unsalted), measuring spoons, and 3 tablespoons of peanut oil.

Pour the peanuts and 1½ tablespoons of peanut oil into the blender. Blend until the mixture is smooth. Add the remaining 1½ tablespoons of peanut oil and blend again.

Taste some straight or try your homemade peanut butter in one of these ways: on toast, on a cracker with a slice of banana or a chunk of sweet pickle, spread on a stick of celery.

Cotton boll

Cotton

LONG AGO, wool was the main fiber used to make cloth in Europe. Then traders returning from Asia brought back cotton robes and tales of a lamb tree. Supposedly the fruit of this tree were small lambs. From the coats of these lambs, the people of the Orient wove beautiful, soft, and very absorbent cloth. Surprisingly, cotton cloth was also brought back by the Spaniards visiting the Aztecs, Mayas, and Incas of the Americas. Cotton plants had developed simultaneously on opposite sides of the earth, and people in both areas had quickly learned to spin these fibers into threads.

Eventually, the people of Europe learned the truth about the lamb plants, and cotton began to be raised and spun along the Mediterranean Sea. Cotton plants can only grow where there are more than 180 warm days, with plenty of sunlight and rain. The most important factor limiting how much cotton people could produce, though, was that it took a lot of time and effort to separate the fibers from the seeds. Cotton fibers actually grow from each seed's protective seed coat. Then in 1793, Eli Whitney, an American inventor, developed the cotton gin to separate the seeds from the cotton fibers mechanically. Cotton quickly became the most important crop in the southern part of the United States.

Today, cotton seeds are also a valuable crop. Oil from these seeds is used to manufacture salad oil, margarine, soap, and cosmetics. The pulp left after the oil has been removed is used as animal food because it is a good source of protein.

RIDDLE

> *The more there is of it, the less you can see. What is it?*
> *Darkness*

Make a Bird Shooer

CROWS AND other seed-eating birds have been attacking crops as long as people have been growing grain. So a never-ending war has been waged. The ancient Egyptians battled pesky quails that attacked their wheat by driving the birds into nets. As sort of a bonus, besides saving their crop, the farmers also had quail for dinner. The ancient Greeks, Romans, and even the Japanese built scarecrows as guardians against the birds. These were sometimes wooden statues and other times straw-stuffed figures. These ancient farmers believed that spirits of protective gods entered these scarecrows to watch over the plants. At a special harvest ceremony, Japanese farmers traditionally gathered all their scarecrows together, stacked offerings of rice cakes and other foods around them, and set the pile on fire. This was their way of freeing the guardian spirits so they could go back to their home for the winter.

Scarecrows have never been very effective at shooing away clever crows, though. So people have continually tried to find more effective ways to keep birds out of the crops. The Zuni Indians of the southwestern United States strung cords made of plant fibers from poles, forming a network of lines above the corn plants. From these they hung bones, rags, anything that would wave or clatter in the wind. In Great Britain, boys and even sometimes girls were sent out to patrol the fields, scaring away birds. Besides waving their arms and throwing stones, the bird shooers used clappers. These were wooden paddles to which two pieces of wood had been loosely bound—one on each side of the paddle. Shaking this back and forth made the wood pieces slap against the paddle with a loud *clap-clap*.

Scarecrow

With an adult partner to help, you could make a wooden clapper. Or follow the directions to make an effective, but less noisy model. You'll need a piece of oak-tag board, two extra-sturdy paper or Styrofoam plates that have at least a half-inch-high edging rim, sharp scissors, and an eighteen-inch-long piece of string.

First, cut a paddle shape about the size of a Ping Pong paddle out of the oak tag. Mark two dots an inch apart about an inch above the

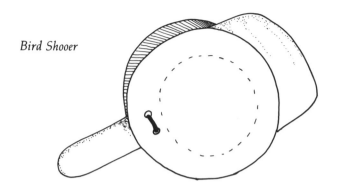
Bird Shooer

paddle handle. Mark two dots an inch apart and about an inch from the edge on the bottom of each plate. Use the pointed tip of the scissors to carefully poke a hole at each dot. Make the holes large enough for the string to slip through easily.

Hold one plate with the bottom facing you and thread the string through both holes. Next, thread both ends through the paddle, and finally thread them through the second plate—the side you would put food on. You'll need to work with the yarn to see just how tightly it should be tied. The two plates should be against the paddle at rest but be able to flop back and forth, slapping into the paddle, when you shake it.

Take your finished clapper outdoors and try it out. Can you startle any birds, making them leave your yard or trees?

In the 1950s, farmers tried using DDT and other poisonous chemicals to repel both insects and birds. These were effective, but by the 1960s people realized that the chemicals were harmful to human consumers too. So farmers went back to using things that wave, glisten in the sun, or make noise to shoo birds away.

Bringing in the Crops

FOR HUNDREDS of years, farmers harvested their grain crop by cutting the stalks with scythes and sickles, tools with big curved blades. The stalks were then bound into bundles called sheaves and stacked in the field until they could be threshed. Threshing is the process of beating the stalks to separate out the grain. Harvesting the grain crop was a slow, difficult, and time-consuming project.

Finally, in the mid-1800s, several people developed machines called reapers to help harvest grain. The first commercially successful reaper was built by Cyrus McCormick. It was pulled by horses, and as the machine moved forward a wheel rolled, driving the machine's moving parts. A reel rotated, and paddles on it pressed the stalks against a four-and-a-half-foot-long vibrating blade. As the grain heads were sliced off, the paddles pushed the stalks onto a platform. A worker, following the reaper, raked the stalks off the platform and still other workers tied the stalks into sheaves. Although it was still a lot of work, cutting the grain and getting it out of the field could now be completed much faster than before, so farmers could raise larger grain crops. The grain still had to be threshed, separated from its hard outer covering, though. Reaping had to be completed within ten days of ripening or the grain was likely to begin to rot.

The invention of the combine was an even bigger help. This machine is called a combine because it was both a harvester, cutting the stalks and removing the grain from the stalks, and a thresher. The first successful model was built by Hiram Moore and John Haskall in the 1830s. It could cut sections of grain more than twenty feet wide. When the grain moved up onto the platform, a feeder carried it to a threshing drum. As the outer hull was removed the grain fell through a grate into a storage tank and the remaining stalks were baled as straw. As many as eighteen to twenty horses were needed to pull these big machines. Although some models used steam-powered engines, it was the internal-combustion engine like those used in automobiles, that finally supplied the power needed to run these big farm machines.

Today, some combines are able to cut a thirty-five-foot wide section of grain in one pass. Special attachments also let combines harvest corn, soybeans, and rice.

Going to Seed

AUTUMN IS the season when many different kinds of plants are producing seeds. Seeds are life packages. They contain an embryo or young plant and a supply of food—everything needed to produce a new plant. Many are also enclosed in a protective covering, a seed coat that allows them to withstand harsh winter weather. A few, such as those from cottonwood trees, must fall on damp soil and start to grow within a few hours or die. Most seeds, though, reach full development in autumn but don't sprout until spring.

More than 250,000 kinds of plants produce seeds—each different in size, color, and structure. Some seeds are real surprise packages. A redwood-tree seed, for example, is tiny—only one-sixteenth of an inch long. But this tiny seed will produce a tree that is likely to be over three hundred feet tall.

Many seeds are travelers that use a variety of getaway techniques to make sure they will land in a place where they have plenty of room to grow. Some ride away on the wind. Some float away on water. And still others hitchhike, snagging a ride on a passing animal.

Here are a few plants whose seeds leave home in autumn.

Maple seeds

Maple Trees

The seeds produced by these trees are nature's helicopters. Each seed is attached to a long papery wing that catches the wind and makes the seed spin. If you can find a maple tree in your area, you can discover for yourself what having wings does for the seeds.

Start by choosing two seeds that are about the same size. Carefully break the wing off one seed. Next hold the two seeds in one hand, stretch your arm up as high as you can, and release the seeds together. You'll discover that the winged seed falls more slowly. This slowed descent gives the wind more time to carry the seed away from the parent tree. And being out from under its parent's shady branches gives the young plant that sprouts from the seed a better chance to grow into a big tree.

How far does a maple seed travel from its parent? Find a maple tree and look around it for winged seeds that have landed. Measure from the seed that is farthest away to the point directly below the end of the tree's branches. Most only travel about a hundred yards, but in a strong steady wind some may fly much farther.

Maples aren't the only trees that produce winged seeds. Ashes, elms, and box elders are among the other trees whose seeds have wings. Scientist call these winged seeds "samaras."

Tumbleweeds

THIS PLANT depends on the wind to spread its seeds, but the whole parent plant moves. Each plant grows from six to twenty inches high and has many branching stems. The tumbleweed's seeds are as tiny as dust, but one plant produces as many as four million seeds. In the fall when the seeds are mature, the tumbleweed plant dries. Eventually, a strong wind tears the plant loose from the soil. Then each gust of wind sends the tumbleweed rolling along, scattering its seeds.

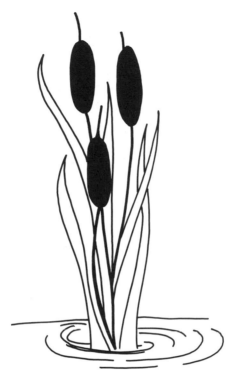

Cattails

THE SEEDS of this plant are attached to silky puffs too. Although they mature in the fall, they remain, clinging in a brown, cigar-shaped cluster, through the winter and spring. When summer at last arrives, the puffs fluff out enough to be carried away by the wind. Cattails, however, grow in marshes and on the edge of shallow ponds. So the seeds usually land in water and float still farther away. Only the few seeds that land on a favorable spot actually sprout and grow into a new cattail plant. Don't worry about cattails becoming extinct, though. Each cattail produces as many as 250,000 seeds.

Sticktights

SOMETIMES CALLED beggar-ticks, the seeds of these plants use the Velcro technique. Each half-inch-long dark brown seed has two sharp prongs. When an animal brushes against the plant, the dried bristly flower head bursts open. Then the seeds stick to the animal's fur. You may have found these seeds hitching a ride on your socks or pant legs.

Mistletoe

THIS PLANT is a parasite, meaning that it can't make food for itself. It has to be able to send its roots into another plant and get food from it. So mistletoe can only grow if its seeds land on a tree's

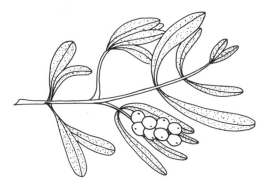

branches or trunk. To make sure this happens, mistletoe seeds are very sticky and are produced inside berries. When birds eat the berries, the seeds stick to their beak. Later, perhaps in another tree the bird rubs its beak against the tree's bark to wipe off the seed. The seed settles into the bark and sprouts, and roots grow into the tree. Or the bird may swallow the seed. Even strong digestive juices don't affect the mistletoe seed's stickiness. So if the bird's droppings land on a branch, the seed can still sprout and begin to grow.

Seed Poppers

TOUCH THE ripe seedpod of a jewelweed and something surprising happens. The sides of the long pod suddenly curl open, shooting out about twenty dark seeds. These plants don't wait for wind, water, or animals to move their seeds. They have their own built-in seed-launching system. As the seedpod matures, it separates into five sections. And as the pod dries, some of the walls shorten more than others, creating a strain where the walls join. Eventually, the slightest pressure causes these seams to rip open. The sections coil up, snapping the seeds out as far as seven feet. No

wonder this plant is sometimes called "touch-me-not."

Wild geraniums and mountain wisteria also launch their own seeds. The peas and beans people grow in their vegetable gardens would do the same thing if allowed to stay on the vines. As the pods dry out, they would twist as they split open, popping out pea and bean seeds as far as several feet.

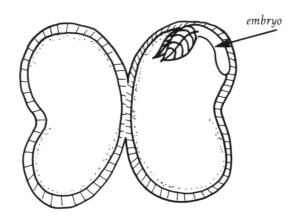

embryo

Peek inside a Seed

FOLLOW THESE directions to see the embryo, baby plant, inside the seed.

1. Get a small package of dried beans from the grocery store. Pick out eleven unbroken beans that are all about the same size.

2. Place ten of the seeds in a glass and use a crayon to mark the top level of the seeds on the glass. Next, add just enough water to cover the seeds. The plant embryo needs water to sprout and begin to grow. Each seed has a tough outer coat to protect it, but a tiny

hole called the micropyle lets water enter more easily than it can through this protective layer. If you look closely, you may be able to see the micropyle.

3. Let the seeds sit overnight and then look at them again. The seeds will appear to be above the level you marked. As they soaked up water, the seeds swelled. Compare one of the soaked seeds to the dry seed to see just how much bigger it has become.

4. Pour off the water and dump the seeds out on a paper towel. Slip the seed coat off one seed and examine it. The seed is in two parts. Carefully separate these parts along their natural dividing line. The two large parts are called the cotyledons. These are the stored food that the young plant would use to start growing. It is also what supplies you with nourishment if you eat the seed. Lying on one of the cotyledons you'll see what looks like a little stem with two tiny leaves on one end. That is the baby plant.

Now that you know how to peek inside, try opening other seeds, such as corn kernels, squash seeds, or peanuts. Do they all have two sections of stored food or do some have only one? In what ways, if any, are the embryos different?

Go on a Seed Hunt

GO SEED hunting outdoors and see how many different kinds of seeds you can find. Observe carefully and try to guess how each seed type travels: by wind, by water, by being launched, or hitching a ride with an animal. Don't forget to check your clothing for seeds. Any you find are obviously hitchhikers.

Next, go seed hunting in your kitchen and at the grocery store. First, look for dried seeds like beans, peas, and popcorn. Coffee and chocolate are made from seeds. Next, look for fruits. A fruit is any part developed by the plant to support the seeds. Sometimes it is fleshy, as in apples and peaches and squash. Or it may be dry, as in walnuts and pecans. Some of what are commonly called vegetables are also really fruits. The seeds may be inside the fruit where you can't see them the way they are in tomatoes, cherries, cucumbers, and watermelons. Or they may be on the outside and easy to spot, the way they are in strawberries and raspberries.

Don't forget to check the spice section too. Pepper, nutmeg, and dill are seeds. Celery seeds and mustard seeds are also often used as spices. What other seeds can you find?

Seedy Art

COLLECT AS many different-looking seeds as you can find, such as squash seeds, popcorn, and different varieties of bean seeds. Choose seeds that are different shapes, different sizes, and different colors. Wash and pat dry any seeds you have removed from fruit.

Then use these seeds to make a mosaic, a picture created by fitting together little pieces to make a completed whole. You'll also need a piece of poster board, a pencil, and white glue.

First, plan your picture and sketch it on the poster board. For the best results, keep the picture simple. Next, divide it into sections. Plan how you will use the different seeds to give color and texture to different sections of your picture.

Then fill in the mosaic one section at a time. Spread a thin, even coat of glue over the section you'll be working on. Press the seeds into the glue one at a time. Work quickly. If the section to be covered is very large, you may only want to spread glue over part of the area at a time.

RIDDLE

What's Dracula's favorite fruit?
Neck-tarines.

Thanksgiving around the World

PEOPLE HAVE celebrated the harvest since earliest times. The ancient Egyptians held an autumn festival in honor of Min, the god they believed made the earth fertile. The Greeks honored Demeter, their goddess of agriculture, with a nine-day celebration. The Romans held a similar holiday in honor of Ceres, their harvest goddess. Their festivities always included sporting events as well as a feast featuring fruits and nuts.

In ancient China, the harvest celebration was called Hhung-

Ch'iu, the birthday of the moon. It was held on the fifteenth day of the eighth moon, a time people call the harvest moon. The Chinese, like farmers everywhere, especially appreciated the full moon during the harvest season because it provided enough light to finish bringing in the crops. The moon's birthday cakes were round (full-moon-shaped) rice cakes prepared with grain from the new harvest. These were served outdoors at a moonlit feast.

Followers of the Jewish religion still observe the harvest festival called Sukkoth, the Feast of the Tabernacles. During this holiday, which lasts eight days, people traditionally build a booth or sukkah. This crude shelter is meant to be a reminder to the Jewish people of the forty years their ancestors wandered in the wilderness before entering the promised land of Canaan.

Although the Pilgrim's harvest celebration held in 1621 is often thought of as the first Thanksgiving in the New World, it wasn't. Native Americans already had a long-standing tradition of celebrating the harvest. And the Jamestown Colony established in 1607 is believed to have held a special harvest church service each year.

President George Washington called for the first national day of Thanksgiving to be celebrated in the United States on November 26, 1789. The event was repeated in November of 1795, but after that the tradition lapsed. The current observance of a national Thanksgiving Day is largely the result of the thirty-year effort of Sarah Josepha Hale. As the editor of *Godey's Lady's Book*, a very popular publication in the United States, she campaigned for the establishment of this holiday. Finally, President Abraham Lincoln proclaimed that the last Thursday in November be set aside for this holiday, and the first official Thanksgiving Day was celebrated in 1863. Canada also celebrates a national Thanksgiving Day, but there this holiday is observed on the second Monday in October.

The Truth about the Pilgrims

THE PILGRIMS are always associated with Thanksgiving, but how much do you really know about the Pilgrims? Take this quiz to test yourself. Then check the answers on page 00. The facts are likely to surprise you.

1.   The *Mayflower* was the only ship the Pilgrims hired to carry them to the New World. True or False.

2.   The Pilgrims were actually separatists or Puritans who chose to move to the New World to be able to practice their religion. True or False.

3.   The Pilgrims funded their move to the New World entirely on their own. True or False.

4.   The Pilgrims originally intended to settle in the Virginia Colonies. True or False.

5.   The Pilgrims named their settlement Plymouth. True or False.

6.   The Pilgrims landed in the spring and quickly cleared land for their crops. True or False.

7. The Pilgrims probably dressed the way they're shown in the picture. True or False.
8. The main weapon used by the Pilgrims was the blunderbuss. True or False.

Answers to The Truth about the Pilgrims

1.   False.   The Pilgrims actually started their journey aboard a ship called the *Speedwell*, which carried them from Holland to England. There, they gained a second ship, the *Mayflower*, and both ships set sail for the New World. However, the *Speedwell* quickly developed problems and was not able to leave England. Some people were forced to remain behind. The rest crowded aboard the *Mayflower*, making 102 people aboard a ship barely ninety feet long.

2.   True.   The Pilgrims were separatists whose religious beliefs were not recognized by the Church of England. When they first left England seeking religious freedom, they only moved as far as Holland. However, they also wanted to continue their traditions and maintain their English heritage, so they became concerned as they saw their children learning to speak Dutch and to observe Dutch customs. Finally, after twelve years, they decided to move to the New World.

3.   False.   The Pilgrims were financed by a group of English businessmen. In return for their trip and the provisions they needed to start their colony, the Pilgrims were to send back furs, fish, and lumber for the merchants to sell.

4.   True.   However, when the *Mayflower* landed in a harbor off the tip of Cape Cod after nearly two months at sea, the people decided to stay there rather than go on.

5.   False.   The spot where the Pilgrims landed had been visited by John Smith of the Virginia Colonies during an earlier expedition. Captain Smith had already named this area Plymouth.

6.   False.   The Pilgrims landed on November 9, and a team of men spent a month exploring before they selected a settlement site. Although they built eleven sturdy houses, the winter was so hard that nearly half the people did not survive. When spring finally did arrive, they didn't have to do much to clear the land for planting, though. The Pilgrims settled where a group of Native Americans called the Patuxet had lived until the entire community was wiped out by a plague.

7.   True.   No one is quite sure why artists began showing Pilgrims wearing black clothes with big buckles and collars. According to historical accounts, buckles weren't fashionable until much later, so the pilgrims probably didn't wear buckles on their shoes, hats, or jackets. Collars were also likely to be of a variety of styles rather than the big white shawl-like collars usually pictured. Men were as likely to wear a soft cap as a big hat and the women probably wore close-fitting caps with their hair tucked underneath. Perhaps most surprising is that the Pilgrims probably didn't always wear black. Their everyday clothes would have been similar to what other people were wearing in England during that period. So historians believe the Pilgrims wore clothing that was red, tan, rusty brown, and even purple.

8.   False.   No one who really wanted to hit anything used a

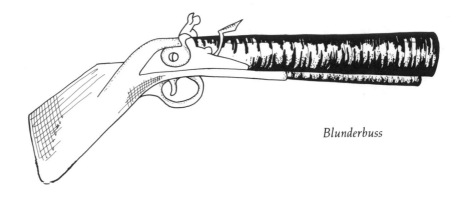

Blunderbuss

blunderbuss. This weapon was an early device for controlling riots—more noise than danger. The Pilgrim men hunted with a straight-barreled gun.

Moving to the New World

WHEN THE Pilgrims packed for their trip to the New World, they took with them the things that would be essential in helping them start their new life. They took along plows, hoes, saws, axes, shovels, nails, fishing hooks, chisels, anvils, kettles, spoons, frying pans, grinding wheels, knives, muskets, and gun powder. They packed food: dried sausage, salt beef, oatmeal, cheese, flour, nuts, beans, apples, and more. They brought enough food to last for the nearly two-month voyage and for the time it would take to get settled. They also brought along seeds to plant. In addition to these necessary items, each family was allowed one trunk in which they could carry along personal possessions.

What if your family was about to move to a "New World"? What if this place didn't have houses or apartments where you could live.

It didn't have any stores full of goods. It didn't even have a pizza parlor that delivered. Make a list of all the things your family would need to take along to live in this new home. Also make a list of the personal items your family would want to carry along in its one trunk.

The Amazing Adventures of Squanto

YOU PROBABLY know that Squanto was a Native American who befriended the Pilgrims and helped them learn to live successfully in the New World. There was a special reason why Squanto chose to help the Pilgrims and why he was able to work with them so well.

When Squanto was about fourteen, a shipload of white men came to trade with his tribe, the Patuxet. When it was time for the men to leave, they took Squanto and several other Indians back to England with them. Sir Fernando Georges, who had sponsored the trading venture, was eager to meet with some Indians. He believed that if he could get firsthand information about the New World—about the climate, the game, the fish, and the native tribes—he would be able to make profitable investments in this region. So upon reaching England, Squanto was taught to speak English in order to be able to answer Sir Georges's questions.

Squanto was well treated and his new life among the English was not unpleasant, but he was homesick. It was nine long years, though, before he was able to find a way to return. At last, he signed on with Captain John Smith, who was on his way to the New World in search of whales and gold. The ship reached its destination safely, but no whales or gold were discovered. So that the trip wouldn't be a total loss, Squanto helped Captain Smith trade for furs and fish. Then he asked permission to leave and started home.

Before he could get back to the Patuxet, though, Squanto was captured again. This time, he was taken from the New World to Spain and sold into slavery. More long years—this time years of hard labor—passed before Squanto was able to escape. He made his way to England once again and this time signed aboard a fishing vessel bound for Newfoundland.

After more months of hard work, Squanto was able to get passage from Newfoundland to the region that is now called New England, his homeland.

This time Squanto made it back to his village, but he found the fields untended and the homes empty. In the nearby village of the Wampanoag, he learned the sad news. While he had been away, his family, his friends, all the people of his village, had died from a terrible disease. He was the last of the Patuxet. Since winter was coming, Squanto stayed with the Wampanoag, but he kept to himself, feeling lonely and grief-stricken.

That spring, word came that new settlers had arrived during the winter and were living in the Patuxet village. Surprised, Squanto went to see for himself. He discovered that the news was true. Small houses now stood where there had once been an Indian village. And white men and women were working the fields that had once supplied food for his family and friends.

Squanto first met the Pilgrims when he acted as translator for Massasoit, chief of the Wampanoag. But when they showed him the baskets of corn (maize) that they had discovered in the village, he remained to show the new settlers how to raise this crop that they knew nothing about. He taught them how to raise beans and pumpkins too. He showed them how to dig for eels in the mud at low tide and where to hunt for moose and turkeys. He helped them tap maple trees for the sweet sap and taught them which plants made good medicine. Although he'd only come to act as a translator, Squanto stayed to become a good friend. It was lucky for the Pilgrims that there was still one Patuxet left and that he had finally come home.

Bounce the Berry

CRANBERRIES ARE one of those foods that just naturally seem to be a part of Thanksgiving feasting. No one knows for sure if the Pilgrims ate these ruby-red berries at the first Thanksgiving, but they have certainly been on North American menus since colonial times. In fact, European settlers learned about cranberries from the Native Americans who used them for food, medicine, and as a dye for cloth.

Cranberries grew abundantly wherever it was swampy as far south as what is now Virginia. Today, cultivated cranberries are

cranberry blossom

cranberries

grown in special fields that have a base of acid soil or peat, a spongy plant material, plenty of water, and a layer of sand. An adequate drainage system is critical to successful cranberry growing because while the plants need lots of water, they cannot tolerate being in standing water. Flooding the fields and then draining them quickly is a method used to control insect pests without insecticides. The bogs must also be flooded immediately if there is a chance of frost. Ice on the bog protects and insulates the sensitive plants.

One of the hardest parts of raising cranberries is harvesting them. For years, this job could only be done by hand or with a special comblike rake. Today, cranberry farmers use a special wet-pick method. The fields are flooded and a machine with big rotating wheels churns up the water. This dislodges the cranberries, which pop to the surface and float. Then workers wading in the bog push the "rafts" of berries into receiving stations.

After they're harvested, it's necessary to test each berry for freshness. A fresh cranberry is hard enough to bounce. In fact, a bounce test is how cranberry-producing companies check their berries. Dropped from a height of about seven inches, cranberries must bounce high enough to clear a barrier. If they can pass this test a total of seven times, the berries are considered fresh enough to be shipped to market.

Try it yourself. Buy some fresh cranberries at the market. (They may only be available at Thanksgiving time in your area.) Then measure up seven inches from a hardwood or tile floor. Drop the berries one by one from this height. Do all the berries bounce the same or do some leap higher? Have a friend help you by dropping the berries while you watch them bounce. Then wash the berries and follow a recipe to make some cranberry relish. This fruit is an excellent source of vitamin C, the vitamin your body needs to stay well and to help wounds heal.

If you want to taste a fresh cranberry, wash one and pop it into your mouth. Don't be surprised if you don't like the taste, though. One of the names given to these berries by Native Americans meant "bitter berry." The Pilgrims mixed cranberries with maple sugar or honey. Read labels and you'll discover that cranberry sauce and cranberry-juice drinks contain sugar to make them taste sweeter.

The National Turkey

OF COURSE you think about having turkey for Thanksgiving dinner, but did you ever consider the turkey as the United States's national bird? Benjamin Franklin thought it should be. The bird that impressed him, though, was the wild turkey, not the tame bird that is raised for its meat.

Wild turkeys are true American natives, once ranging over a territory that covers what is now thirty-nine states from Canada to Mexico and west to Wisconsin. They're also clever enough to hide from enemies and powerful enough to fight if they can't escape. Big males or toms average four feet tall, weigh about sixteen pounds, and have sharp two-inch-long spurs on their legs for fighting. Wild turkeys are strong fliers, capable of traveling at speeds up to fifty-five miles per hour for short distances. They've also been clocked running as fast as twenty-five miles per hour.

Wild turkeys are omnivores, which means they'll eat almost anything. They travel in family flocks, hunting for food on the ground during the day and sleeping in trees at night. The traditional turkey's "gobble, gobble" is the male's courting call. Only the adult male turkey or tom has the familiar "beard" and only a courting bird fans out its tail feathers. The female turkey or hen builds a crude nest in the undergrowth for her brood of ten to twelve eggs.

Deprived of much of its habitat by settlers clearing the land and killed off by diseases brought in with domestic birds, the flocks of wild turkeys were greatly reduced by the late 1800s. Only the efforts to protect and breed these birds that were carried out in this century saved them from becoming extinct.

Every season seems to have its own special holidays. Halloween is a fall holiday that's full of spooky fun. And Halloween is what the next chapter is all about. You won't want to miss the action!

3.
HAPPY
HALLOWEEN

Celebrating Samhain

THE LAST day of October is traditionally a day for dressing up and pretending to be ghosts and goblins and witches and such. It's generally a time for collecting treats and having fun. But the origins of this good-natured autumn event reveal that what is now done playfully was once serious business.

The ancient Celts, a group of people who lived in what is now England, Ireland, and France, held a festival called Samhain on October 31 to mark the end of summer. The dramatic seasonal changes that occurred at this time of the year seemed mystical, and so this holiday was considered full of magic.

The Celts believed that on Samhain night the souls of all those who had died the previous year returned in animal bodies to visit their old homes. Fearfully, the people extinguished all their kitchen fires so their homes were dark. Then they gathered in the center of their villages as the Druids, their priests, lit a huge bonfire of oak branches. The people tossed food and even living animals into this fire as gifts to their gods. More bonfires were lit on the surrounding hills as a further effort to keep the spirits away. In the morning, the Celts took glowing coals from the dying bonfire home to start new

Bonfire

kitchen fires. And the Druids studied the ashes to tell what events the next year would hold. November 1, the day after Samhain, marked the beginning of the New York to them.

Mixing Customs

THE ANCIENT Romans, who moved in and took control of the land occupied by the Celts, continued to celebrate the Roman festivals they were used to observing. However, they were aware of the local customs and gradually the Roman and Celtic traditions began to merge. The Romans also had a holiday for honoring the dead, so they easily accepted the celebration of Samhain for this tradition. To this, though, the Romans added their fall harvest customs. They were used to honoring Pomona, goddess of fruits and trees, with a feast followed by games and races.

Later, as Christianity spread and grew in strength, the Church attempted to eliminate these pagan customs by replacing them with Christian holidays. All Saints' Day, a day set aside to honor any saint without a specific church day, was moved from May to November 1. November 2 became All Souls' Day in memory of the dead.

Despite the Church's strong opposition, many people continued to observe the long-established traditions. Gradually, though, many of the old customs mingled with the new. Some of the old beliefs were also maintained but given new, Christian meanings. For example, bonfires continued to be built on October 31, but now the fires were lit to keep the devil away.

Since November 1 was often called All Hallows' Day, October 31 became known as All Hallows' Even. This was eventually shortened to Halloween.

Trick-or-Treating

THIS JUST-for-fun custom of dressing up and going door-to-door to collect goodies is another tradition with a mixed Christian and pagan beginning. In ancient Ireland, people wearing masks formed processions and went door-to-door begging for food. If a person refused to give out food, Muck Olla, one of the Celtic gods, would be angered and see to it that the coming year wasn't a good one. So everyone gave generously. Later, in Christian churches, people wore costumes to participate in special pageants presented on All Saints' Day. Those in the pageant dressed as saints while other members of the congregation dressed as demons. On All Souls' Day, poor people

went "a-souling". This meant that they went door-to-door, collecting a treat in return for promising to pray for family members who had died.

Eventually these serious customs became ones that were performed simply for fun. And just as old customs gradually change, today trick-or-treating has a new twist. In many cities, children are invited to stop by local hospitals after trick-or-treating to have their goodies x-rayed. Some children have been seriously hurt by eating treats into which unkind people have inserted razor blades, pins, or other sharp objects. Of course, the best way to stay safe when you trick-or-treat is to only visit people your family knows and trusts.

Who Is That Masked Person—Really?

PUT ON a mask and you not only look like someone or something else, you feel different. Halloween is one of those times during the year when people still enjoy putting on a false face. Masks, though, were once a very important, and serious, part of many cultures throughout the world.

Sometimes masks were a way of dealing with the forces of evil or nature so they could be controlled. In Sri Lanka, for example, the people used to believe that demons caused diseases. So when someone was seriously ill, a person wearing a demon mask appeared and then was driven away. In this way, it was hoped that illness would be overcome and the person made well once again.

Kwakiatl Indian Mask

The Iroquois Indians of the eastern United States and Canada had people put on carved wooden masks of strangely twisted faces with big lips. These masked characters supposedly became the messengers of corn, beans, and squash. And by dancing with these masked spirits, the Indian farmers believed they could ensure a good harvest of these important food crops.

Although it's now just for fun, an annual pretend battle is still staged in Imst, Austria, between masked spirits of winter and spring, fighting for control of nature.

Masks also helped people pass on customs and legends. The Kwakiutl tribe, which inhabited what is now Vancouver, British Columbia, used masked figures to act out legends about the history of the world. Many of the Kwakiutl masks were beautifully carved out of wood and had parts that moved when ropes were pulled.

Initiation rites when boys became men and girls became women and the ceremonies of secret societies often involved masks. In New Guinea, boys wearing masks were sent into a monster's mouth. This was actually only the door of a hut decorated to look like a monster's mouth, but they emerged from the hut as men. The Hopi and Zuni Indian tribes of the southwestern United States still have *kachinas*. These masked figures, representing little gods or spirits, perform secret rituals, often in a *kiva* or second lodge, to help crops grow, to fight off diseases, and to maintain discipline. Masks were also frequently put on the dead to protect and assist them as they entered the next world.

RIDDLE

What do you call the land where
monsters live?

A terror-tory.

Make a Monster of Yourself

OF COURSE you'll want a costume for Halloween. Below is a suggested list of some of the more famous ghouls you might want to imitate. This is the season to be creative. So dig through the closets, drawers, and cupboards for items you might use. Be sure to get permission, though, from whoever owns these goodies before you go to work. If you'll be going out in the dark trick-or-treating, be sure to pay close attention to the safety tips.

Vampire
Count Dracula
Witch or Warlock (male witch) Cyclops
Devil Skeleton
Mummy Alien
Werewolf Black Cat (witch's friend)
Ghost Bat
Frankenstein

Safety Tips:

1. Carry a flashlight.
2. Wear plenty of white or include strips of reflective tape (available at stores that carry supplies for bike riders and joggers).
3. Be sure your costume is short enough and loose enough that you can walk and climb stairs easily without tripping.
4. Paint your face using water-based makeup, grease-paint (the kind actors use), or colored sunblocks rather than masks that could block your vision.
5. Go with an adult or in a group; go only to houses of people your family knows and trusts.

Jack-o'-Lanterns

HALLOWEEN WOULDN'T be Halloween without jack-o'-lanterns. The custom of these eerie candlelit night-lights began, so the story is told, long, long ago.

There was once a man named Jack O'Grady who was so selfish and so mean that people said he was worse than the devil. But Jack was also very clever. When the devil came to take his soul one Halloween night, Jack tricked the devil into letting him live another year. It was the next Halloween as Jack was walking home on a lonely dark road that the devil caught up with him.

"I've come for your soul," the devil announced with a grin. "The gates of hell are open, so you and I can go right on in."

"Whoa!" Jack said, thinking fast. "There's no rush. Wouldn't you like to have one of those shiny red apples hanging on that tree over there. I've been told that they're the sweetest apples in the whole country. Why don't you climb up and pick us each an apple before we go. I'd sure hate to go to hell hungry."

Now the devil decided he was a bit hungry too. "Why not," he agreed, and up the tree he went.

But no sooner had the devil climbed up than Jack whipped out his pocketknife and carved a cross on the tree's trunk. Everyone knows that the devil is terribly afraid of crosses, so he was trapped.

"You've tricked me," snapped the devil.

"Indeed," Jack giggled and laughed. "And I won't let you down till you promise to spare my soul for ten more years."

The devil held out for a bit, but at last he gave in. That, however, was the end of Jack's luck. For before the next year was up, Jack died. The angels, of course, turned Jack away from heaven because of his evil life. So Jack marched down to hell.

"Ho!" The devil laughed. "Do you think I'll let you in? Not now, not nine years from now. Not ever! That will teach you to play tricks on me."

Jack moaned: "If I can't go to heaven and I can't go to hell, where can I go?"

The devil shrugged. "You'll have to roam the earth."

"At least give me a light," pleaded Jack.

Chuckling, the devil tossed Jack a glowing-hot coal. Jack put the coal in a turnip so he wouldn't burn his hands and started off.

Poor Jack, they say, has been wandering ever since. Have you ever seen a small, flickering light moving through the dark on Halloween night? That's Jack. He's still looking for a place to rest.

Carve a Bogie

TODAY, AS in the past, people in Ireland and Scotland often carve jack-o'-lanterns out of turnips. These little lanterns are also called "bogies."

To carve a bogie for yourself, just follow the steps below. You may want to ask an adult to work with you on this project. You'll

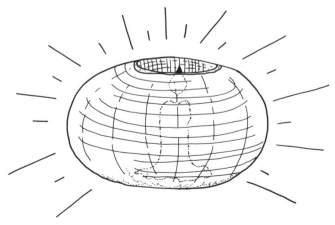

need a turnip (choose the largest one you can find at the grocery store), some newspapers, a knife, and a candle stub.

1. Cover your work area with the newspapers. Then slice a thin piece off the root end of the turnip to make that end flat. This will let you sit your bogie down on the table.

2. Next, slice the top off the turnip. Use the knife to dig away the center. The whole turnip is one solid mass rather like a potato. So you will have to carve away slowly, being careful not to make the walls too thin. Also be careful not to poke through the bottom of the turnip.

3. Finally, push the candle stub into the hollowed-out turnip. If necessary, cut off the stub. The top of the wick should be below the turnip rim.

4. Take your bogie outdoors and have your adult partner hold and light it. The light will glow through the sheer turnip walls.

Grow Your Own Giant Jack-o'-Lanterns

WHEN THE great numbers of Irish people who had moved to the United States in the mid-1800s celebrated Halloween, they found something even better than turnips for making lanterns. Pumpkins were not only much bigger, they were also easier to carve. Inside the hard shell there was a soft pulp that could easily be scooped out.

There are two basic varieties of pumpkins: stock and cheese.

Cheese pumpkins are smaller, more yellow, and their pulp is considered tastier than stock pumpkins. So cheese pumpkins are usually grown to eat. Stock pumpkins, on the other hand, are big and orange—classic jack-o'-lantern material. In fact, some of these giants may weigh as much as two hundred pounds.

To raise one of these giants for yourself, you'll need seeds for Big Max, Connecticut Field, or Jack-o'-Lantern pumpkins. You'll also need lots of growing space. The vines of the plants that produce these big pumpkins spread out thirty feet or more. And this space will need to be in the sun; the growing plants need about six hours of sunlight every day.

If you have a suitable place to grow your own pumpkins, work up the soil until it is very crumbly. Then heap up a low mound about six feet across and plant four seeds spaced in a small circle near the center of the hill.

Pumpkins are ninety-percent water and they need lots of water to grow, so keep the soil moist and weed-free. Also add fertilizer to the water at least every other week. When the plants blossom, there will be two kinds of flowers: male and female blooms. A pumpkin will develop below each female blossom. So to help your plants produce the biggest possible pumpkin, pluck off all but one female blossom on each vine.

female flower bud

male flower bud

Some growers use this trick to encourage stock pumpkin plants to produce even bigger-than-normal pumpkins. A slit is cut in the vine about three inches from the developing pumpkin. Then a wick of cotton cloth is inserted into the slit. The free end of the wick is kept in a pan of sugar water (add one tablespoon of sugar for every cup of water) or milk. The supply of liquid is refilled as needed or if the milk sours. Does this trick work? You'll have to try it for yourself to find out.

Pumpkin Faces

THE FACE you create won't last as long as the ones carved on Mount Rushmore. In fact, carved pumpkins begin to decay in about four days. But your carving will be a work of art just the same. So first make sketches on scrap paper to decide how you want your jack-o'-lantern to look—smiling, frowning, toothy, funny. When you're ready to carve, draw the outline for the lid and the face on the pumpkin with a marking pen.

Next, cover the work area with newspapers and have an adult

partner work with you to cut the lid out of the hard pumpkin shell. Use a big spoon and your hands to scoop out the pulp.

Notice that each string is attached to a seed. Separate the seeds from the pulp and save them for the "Seedy Treat" recipe.

Before you carve the eyes, nose, and mouth on your pumpkin, take time to try this. Once all the pulp has been removed, set a votive candle (a candle that comes in its own container) inside the pumpkin. (You can use a candle stub, but a votive candle is easier to set inside the slippery pumpkin.) Have your adult partner light the candle. Then put the lid on the pumpkin, making sure it fits snugly. Plug gaps with modeling clay. Wait one minute, then take the lid off. If the candle has not gone out, put the lid back on and wait two minutes. Repeat, adding one minute each time until you lift the lid and discover that the candle flame has stopped burning.

Now light the candle one more time, but leave the lid off the pumpkin this time. Keep watching it for the amount of time that the candle burned with the lid on. You will see the candle won't go out this time. This is because to burn, the candle needs oxygen from the air. Without any holes to let fresh air enter the pumpkin, the flame quickly uses up the available oxygen once the lid is sealed. The eyes, nose, and mouth you carve will not only give your jack-o'-lantern personality, they'll also let in oxygen so your lantern will keep on glowing brightly on Halloween night.

Seedy Treat

PUMPKIN SEEDS make a tasty and healthful snack. Pumpkin seeds are a high energy food—high in protein, minerals, and fiber—and low in sodium.

To prepare this treat, wash the seeds and preheat the oven to 250°F. Next mix the seeds with two tablespoons of vegetable oil. Spread the seeds on a cookie sheet and bake for thirty minutes. Let them cool completely. Then munch!

Witches and Wizards

ORIGINALLY EITHER a man or a woman could be a witch. Later, the words *wizard* and *warlock* came to mean a male witch. Whether a witch or a wizard, the person is considered to have magical powers—especially evil powers. And for centuries, people believed that witches and wizards could actually make things happen. If someone got sick, bread dough didn't rise, or a plague ruined the crops, everyone knew who to blame. Of course, people also turned to witches and wizards for a little magical assistance. Love potions and charms, for example, were purchased in the hopes of attracting the attentions of someone special.

Witchcraft is generally considered simply superstition rather than real magic. However, from the fifteenth through the

Witch

seventeenth centuries, people took a very different view of witches. The Christian Church declared that witches and wizards were led by the devil and posed a serious threat. Books were written to help witch-hunters find these evil creatures. And hundreds of people accused of being witches were executed. The most famous witch-hunt occurred in Salem, Massachusetts, in 1592, when several little girls accused Tituba, a black slave woman, of attacking them with evil magic. As panic spread, more and more people were accused of being witches. Because there are no real witches, all nineteen of the poor people executed as witches in Massachusetts during that witch-hunt were innocent victims.

RIDDLE

Why do witches ride on brooms?

Brooms are cheaper than vacuum cleaners.

The Mean, the Bad, and the Nasty

MONSTERS, GHOULS, and goblins are only fantasy creatures. But there are some real-life animal meanies to watch out for. Some produce a poison that they use to capture their prey and also for defense. Others are especially strong. Some have powerful jaws and a wicked set of teeth. Still others just have a mean disposition and are likely to attack for no reason at all. Whatever way they got their bad reputation, it's a good thing to know about these nasty characters. And if you happen to be in their habitat or home turf, you had better beware!

Scorpions

THIS IS one creature who makes a stand tail-first for a reason. The scorpion's long tail is tipped with a curved sting that is connected to two large venom glands. When the stinger strikes home, strong tail muscles inject a powerful dose of this poison. Scorpions are capable of stinging repeatedly and are poisonous as soon as they're born. The poison they produce affects the heart and breathing rates.

Luckily, scorpions are not aggressive by nature. They simply do what they have to do to protect themselves and to catch an insect or a spider for dinner. Active mainly at night, they don't hesitate to hunt in houses as well as outdoors, though. So if you live in tropical or even subtropical regions, think twice about walking barefoot in the dark.

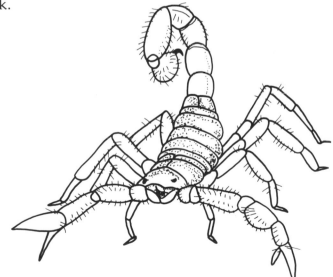

Lionfish

THESE TROPICAL coral-reef fish are so beautiful that they're sometimes kept in saltwater aquariums. But watch out! Some of this fish's lovely, feathery fins are actually stiff, sharp spines. And each spine has an elongated venom gland cloaked in a thin covering of skin. When touched, the spine punctures the skin and venom is ejected into the wound.

For any fish small enough to be swallowed, the lionfish is more than dangerous—it's deadly. A lionfish has a huge appetite and a huge mouth. Opening wide, a lionfish can easily gulp down another fish a third its own size.

Great White Sharks

IT HAS a mouthful of three-inch-long razor-sharp teeth and jaws strong enough to rip a watermelon-sized bite out of its prey. No wonder they called this animal "Jaws" in the movie.

Eating, in fact, is the entire focus of a great white's life, so luckily its teeth are always at their best. While each tooth only lasts about ten days, the shark's mouth is basically a tooth factory with at least five rows of teeth lying flat, in reserve, behind the one or two rows standing upright. So when a tooth is shed, there's always a ready replacement.

Since eating is so important to the great white, it's no wonder that the shark's senses are especially tuned to locating food. While sight isn't its best sense, the shark's big eyes are good at spotting something moving within a hundred feet. And what they can't see, they can "hear" and "smell." Sharks are capable of sensing low-frequency vibrations, which can mean schools of fish or a wounded animal floundering in the water. They can also detect blood in the water as far as a quarter mile away. Special sensory openings in the shark's snout even let it sense the natural electrical impulses given off by moving animals. So the great white shark is well equipped to locate prey even if it can't see it.

Black Widow Spiders

MOST SPIDERS are helpful because they eat insect pests. Some, however, like this one are also dangerous because their bite is poisonous. Black widows are small black spiders with a red hourglass shape on their abdomen. The females are about the size of a marble; the males are about as big as a small pea. These spiders got their name because the females often kill the males after they mate. Black widows—males as well as females—can also kill people, however. The poison they inject affects the nervous system, causing severe pain, nausea, and shortness of breath. Children are most seriously affected because the poison can cause the breathing process to stop. So if you're bitten, seek help immediately. An antivenom to counteract the effect of the spider's poison is available.

Are you wondering if there are any black widows where you live? Probably. These spiders are at home throughout most of the world from Canada to South America, Africa, Europe, Asia, and Australia. They live in every state of the United States except Hawaii and Alaska. Fortunately, though, black widow spiders only bite if disturbed. So if you see one, leave it alone!

Fire Ants

SPREADING LIKE wildfire, these pesky ants are believed to have first slipped into the United States aboard a ship carrying lumber from Brazil in the early 1940s. Now, two-to-three-foot-high fire-ant mounds dot much of the southeastern states—proof that these ants are spreading.

Besides eating farm crops, fire ants are quick to attack animals and people. When disturbed, the angry ant usually bites to hang on. Then it stings repeatedly with the retractable stinger on the tip of its abdomen. In addition to leaving painful blisters, the venom

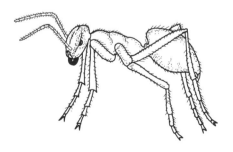

injected by these stings can cause nausea, fever, and even breathing problems.

So far, chemical pesticides have not been very effective in stopping fire ants. The only real barrier to their spread in the United States has been the weather. Fire ants aren't able to survive where winter temperatures frequently drop below 10°F. However, that means that fire-ant colonies are likely to spread eventually as far north as New Jersey in the east and Washington in the west.

African Killer Bees

THIS SPECIES of honeybee doesn't have a more deadly sting than other honeybees, but they're a lot more likely to get upset and attack. And when one African bee is killed, it releases an alarm scent that signals other bees. Sometimes hundreds, even thousands, of bees will join in the attack.

The spread of African bees also has a disastrous effect on the honeybee industry and agriculture in general. When African bees

move into an area, they quickly take over existing honeybee colonies, killing the less agressive bee residents. African bees just naturally collect less nectar, so they do less to help pollinate plants, and they produce less honey. They also often build their hives in the open, attached to tree limbs, where they can be more easily damaged.

Unfortunately, African bees are moving into the United States. This especially aggressive strain of honeybees first entered the Americas in 1956. That year some of the bees escaped from an agricultural experiment being conducted to increase honey production in São Paulo, Brazil. Slowly, ever since, the African killer bees have been moving northward at a rate of about two hundred to three hundred miles each year.

Cobras

YOU MAY have seen this snake in the movies rising from a basket to perform a wiggling "dance" for a snake charmer. Don't be fooled into thinking the snake likes working with people. Cobras are never friendly. Sometimes growing as much as eighteen feet long, they're the biggest poisonous snakes in the world. They're fearless and their poison is likely to be deadly.

If surprised, cobras will strike without warning. Normally, though, these snakes issue a spectacular threat. When alarmed, a cobra rears up, and a big snake may raise its head five or six feet off the ground. Hissing loudly, the snake then spreads the special expandable ribs in its neck into a hood.

Like other poisonous snakes, cobras have two fangs, sharp teeth that act like hypodermic needles, to inject poison when they bite. Some types of cobras are also capable of "spitting" their poison, though. They always seem to aim at the enemy's eyes and with amazing accuracy can strike their target from as far as eight feet away.

Cobras live in Africa and Asia and normally hunt mice and rats in fields. They also often hide near houses, which makes them dangerous to people.

Mosquitoes

THIS SNEAKY villain flies through the night and alights so softly that its victim isn't aware of its presence. Even if it is discovered, the slap usually comes too late. The mosquito has already bitten, inserting its long, strawlike proboscis or mouth and sucking up a little blood. At the same time, the mosquito injects a little saliva to

keep the blood flowing freely. This not only leaves an itchy, red welt because people are usually allergic to it, but the saliva may also contain disease organisms. These may eventually make the person very ill or even kill them. Mosquitoes are known to transmit such diseases as malaria and yellow fever.

Actually, not all mosquitoes are bloodsuckers. Male mosquitoes live on plants and don't have mouth parts capable of piercing skin. So only female mosquitoes bite. In fact, in some species, females are incapable of laying their eggs until they've taken a blood meal.

Most mosquitoes deposit their eggs in still water. Draining swamps and cleaning up junk where puddles of water can form can help control the mosquito population. Bats, swifts, swallows, and dragonflies are also natural mosquito controllers, eating lots of these insects daily.

Wolverines

THESE ANIMALS are proof that the best defense is being offensive. Resembling a miniature bear, wolverines are not only ferocious, they also stink. Whenever wolverines feel threatened—or for no reason other than that they feel mean—they produce a strong, skunklike odor. That's why they're sometimes called "skunk bears."

Wolverines are about three feet long with a low-to-the-ground body and short powerful legs. They have glossy blackish-brown fur with a yellowish to reddish stripe down their back, small beady eyes, and enormous appetites. A wolverine will eat almost anything—berries, birds' eggs, insects, small animals, and even animals several times bigger than itself. Wolverines are famous for being ferocious and clever. In order to tackle big prey, for example, they will climb trees and ambush the passing animal by jumping on its back.

Once wolverines roamed throughout much of Europe, North America, and Asia. Now, though, because so much of the forested land has been cleared, their range has been greatly limited.

The Truth about Vampires

DESPITE ANY scary tales you may have heard about Dracula, the only real vampires never become people. They're strictly bats.

More agile by far than the average bat, which can only move gracefully when in flight, vampire bats can dart across the ground. In fact, they can use their wrists and feet to hop, walk, and sneak up on an unsuspecting—often sleeping—victim in the dark. The bat licks the spot it's going to bite, shearing away any hair. Then it bites, using its large, sharp incisors. As this wound fills with blood, the vampire bat laps up the blood with its tongue. And as it drinks, a

Vampire Bat

little of its saliva drips into the wound. A special chemical in the bat's saliva prevents the blood from clotting for as long as the bat continues lapping.

Each bat may drink about half its own weight in blood, but that's still only about an ounce. A more serious threat is that vampire bats are often carriers of rabies, a deadly virus disease.

Vampire bats feed mainly on animals such as cattle and live in tropical parts of Central and South America. They also represent only a fraction of one percent of all the kinds of bats in the world. While many people think bats look creepy and that their habit of flying at night and sleeping hanging upside down wrapped in their cloaklike wings makes them seem spooky, most bats are really very helpful. Many bats are insect eaters and, help to control insect pests. Other, nectar-eating bats are important night pollinators of plants.

RIDDLE

> *How are all vampires related to each other?*
>
> *They're all blood brothers.*

Real Dragons

THE DRAGONS described in legends were mean and usually giant beasts. Most were also ugly, with claws, a forked tongue, a scaly body, and a spiked tail. They breathed fire. Komodo dragons don't breath fire, but they're impressive creatures just the same. Largest of all the lizards in the world today, they may grow to be nearly nine feet long and weigh over two hundred pounds. However, don't expect to find one of these dragons just anywhere. They only live on Komodo, an island in the Indian Ocean just north of Australia.

Like other reptiles, Komodo dragons hatch from eggs. Youngsters, only eighteen inches long, usually spend their first year high in trees. There they eat insects and birds' eggs and hide from anything that might eat them. When they're about three feet long, the dragons move to the ground. Like their relatives, the snakes, Komodo dragons have pointed tongues that they flick out. Then they tuck the tip into a smelling organ in the roof of their mouth. This way they constantly check for the presence of prey and danger.

Adult dragons will eat almost anything that moves, from

grasshoppers and rats to deer and even wild buffalo. They have razor-sharp claws and teeth with a serrated edge capable of quickly slicing up big chunks of food. Also like snakes, Komodo dragons are able to disconnect their lower jaws, making it possible to swallow very large bites.

Eyes That Glow in the Dark

YOU'VE PROBABLY seen a cat's eyes glow in the dark. You may have thought it looked eerie or spooky. For the animal, though, it means good night vision for hunting. Here's how it happens.

Animals, such as cats and owls, which are active at night, have eyes especially adapted for seeing when there is very little available light. First, these animals have large eyes with pupils that are able to open extra wide. Pupils, the dark spot in the center of each eye, are actually openings—rather like windows—that let light enter the eyes. For the best night sight, some animals also have a special mirrorlike layer called the *tapetum lucidum* behind their retina.

The retina is the layer at the back of the eye that contains light-sensitive cells. When light entering the eye strikes these cells, they respond by sending signals to the brain. Almost instantly, the brain

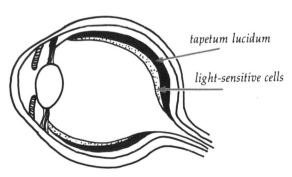

tapetum lucidum

light-sensitive cells

analyzes and interprets these messages, and the animal becomes aware of "seeing." Not all the light that enters the eye strikes light-sensitive cells as it passes through the retina, though. But in animals whose eyes have a tapetum, there's a second chance. The mirrorlike layer bounces any light that reaches it back through the retina. This bounced light is what makes the animal's eyes appear to glow. More importantly, it helps the animal see in very dim light.

Boning Up on Bones

IT'S NO wonder that skeletons, the hard bony body framework of animals, have long been associated with Halloween. Bones are slow to decay, lasting for years after the rest of the animal's soft body parts have rotted away. If you found a skeleton, would you be able to identify the animal by looking at its bones? Here are the bare-bone facts on some skeletons you might find.

If you find a complete skeleton that has more than a hundred vertebrae, or segments, to its backbone, with attached ribs but no legbones, it belonged to a snake. Snakes move by wiggling and gliding, and the numerous vertebrae are designed to slip easily against each other.

Here are the skeletons of two flying animals, a bird and a bat. Can you tell which one belongs to the bat?

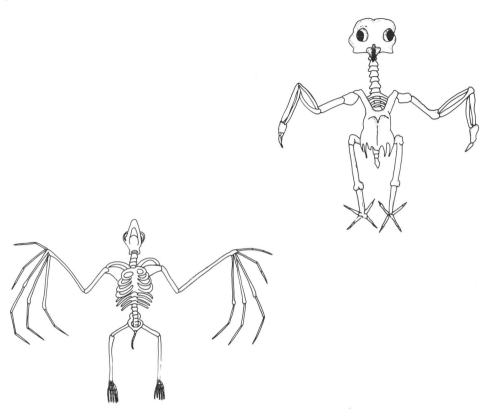

If you guessed the one on the left, you're correct. One easy-to-spot difference is the long, thin fingers. A bird's wings are made up of feathers that spread when the wing is open, so there is no supporting, handlike framework. A bat's wings are skin stretched between the fingerlike supports. Birds also have a much bigger breastbone than bats to support their large flight muscles. And, unlike bats, a bird's hipbones are joined to the backbones. This structure gives a bird the strength needed to support its weight when it lands.

Of course, another noticeable difference between a bird's skeleton and a bat's can be found in the skull or head. Birds have beaks. Depending on the type of food they eat, different kinds of birds have very different-looking beaks.

Chickens peck seeds from the dirt. So they have short, stocky beaks, which are just right to pick up and crack open seeds. Owls are hunters. They have strong curved beaks to tear meat off the bones of mice and other small animal prey. Notice that the owl's skull also has big holes or sockets in its skull for its large eyes—perfect for spotting food in very dim light.

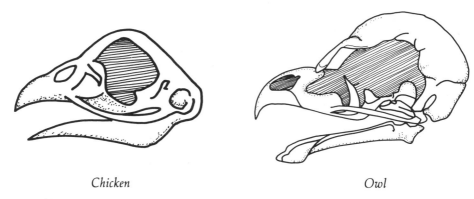

Chicken   *Owl*

The spine or backbone, feet, and legbones will help you identify a frog's skeleton. Usually less than ten vertebrae long, its short stiff spine helps it make big leaps. Look closely and you'll also see that the foot, lower legbones, and upper legbone are all about the same length. These unfold in turn during the jump, providing the needed springboard push.

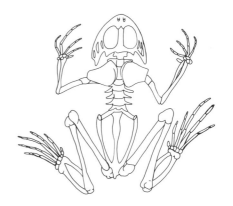

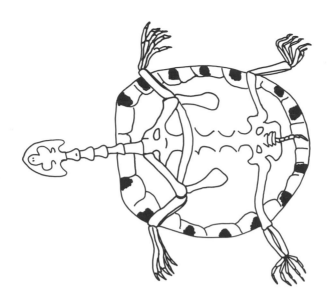

Even if you don't find any other part of the skeleton except the spine, you'll know this animal is a turtle. Only turtles have some of their vertebrae attached with the ribs to the shell.

Here's another skeleton that's tough to miss. Although it has a skull and vertebrae, even these bones are unique. This skeleton, complete with fins, belongs to a fish.

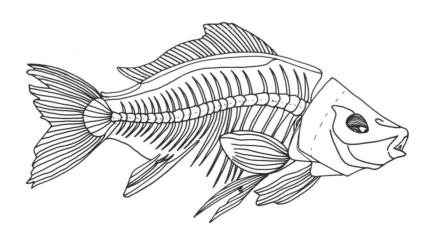

Super Big, Super Old Bones

IMAGINE FINDING a bone eight feet long! That was the size of the giant shoulder blade Jim Jensen found in Dry Mesa quarry in western Colorado. He also found several neck vertebrae nearly five feet long. So far, the whole skeleton has not been found, but these bones are believed to have belonged to one of the biggest dinosaurs that ever lived.

Actually, these bones aren't like the bones in your body. They're fossils. Bones become fossils when, after the animal's soft body parts have rotted away, minerals from the soil replace the original bone material. This usually happens very slowly as water seeps through the bone while it's buried. Like most fossilized dinosaur bones, these giant ones were probably buried about sixty-five million years ago.

Finding fossilized dinosaur bones is like finding the pieces of a puzzle. The rock material surrounding the bone must be carefully chipped away. Then the individual bones are coated in plaster and wrapped in cloth to protect them while they are shipped to museums or laboratories. Finally, the plaster is removed, the bones are cleaned, and the skeleton—as much as had been found—is pieced together. Seeing the assembled skeleton helps scientists predict what the actual dinosaur may have been like.

Based on the fossil bones Jim Jensen discovered, that dinosaur may have been as much as fifty feet tall.

It's Party Time

PEOPLE HAVE been celebrating Halloween with festivals and parties for centuries. So invite a group of your friends to join you on this holiday. Then try the activities below and let science help you make your party sensational.

Snap an Apple

THE ANCIENT Celts and Romans thought apples were magical fruit. So it was no wonder that apples were a part of Halloween celebrations. One popular game that developed from this tradition in Great Britain was apple-snapping. Originally, a rope was tied to the center of a stick and hung from the ceiling. Next, an apple was

stuck on one end of the stick and a candle was attached to the other end. When the candle was lit, the stick was started twirling. Contestants then tried to snatch away the apple without getting burned. This very dangerous game was eventually replaced by bobbing for apples.

To bob for apples, you'll need a large tub full of water. Scrub one apple for each person participating. Then set these afloat. To play, each person in turn will need to kneel over the tub, and with their hands behind their back, work to snatch up an apple in their teeth. Time each player. Whoever succeeds in the shortest amount of time wins.

Grab Some Guts

SIGHT IS the sense people depend on most for clues about the world around them. So if someone is only allowed to use their sense of touch, it's possible to play a funny and spooky Halloween trick on them. You can make them believe they're touching some gruesome body parts—the remains of some poor unfortunate victim. All they'll really be touching, of course, is a number of different food items. Before you can set the scene and play this trick, however, you'll need to prepare the ghoulish fare.

Carefully peel the skin off at least six large grapes to "be" eyeballs. Or if you find this too difficult, use large unpitted olives. Next, cook up a package of large manicotti pasta tubes to simulate pieces of the victim's intestine. Peel one large firm tomato for the heart and cook up three hot dogs for fingers. You'll need candy corn for teeth. Prepare two envelopes of unflavored gelatin following the directions on the box and let this mixture set until firm to be blood.

When the items are ready, place each on an aluminum pie plate or sturdy paper plate. If possible, set the plates out in a room that is separate from the rest of the party. Then plan to have your guests cover their eyes with blindfolds while you guide them through your special, spooky chamber. Or hide each plate inside a box and cut a slot that is just big enough to reach through and touch what's inside. Either way, the important thing is to keep your guests from spying what they touch. Finally, set the scene by telling a ghastly tale about how the victim came to be in this frightful state. Then invite your guests to come "feel" the remains. When everyone's had a turn, reveal the items for what they really are.

Bend a Bone

IS IT magic? No, but your party guests don't have to know that. Just follow these steps to prepare for this trick.

1. Save a wishbone or a legbone from a chicken and clean it well.
2. Place the bone in a quart jar or bowl and cover it with vinegar.
3. Let the bone sit overnight or until it bends easily.
4. Rinse the bone off and dry it.

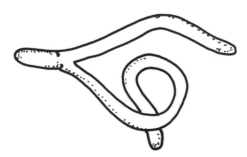

When you're ready to present this trick, explain that you know a magic spell that can make a bone bend. With this, hold up the bone and say something that sounds magical. Then bend the bone forward, backward, and from side to side. Of course, the bone has actually become flexible because the vinegar, a weak acid, has broken down the calcium in the bone. Calcium is one of the elements that combine to make bones hard.

Make Ghostly Noises

TO PRODUCE some really strange, out-of-this world sounds, just follow these directions.

First, you'll need a block of dry ice. Ask an adult to get the ice for you and store it in a cooler. Dry ice is inexpensive and available at many stores that sell ice cream, milk, or canned soft drinks. It's frozen carbon dioxide rather than frozen water and it's much colder than regular ice. Never touch dry ice with your bare hands, this extra-cold ice could injure your skin.

When you're ready to create noises, fill a glass with hot tap water. Take the lid off the cooler, put on an oven mitt, and pick up a large metal serving spoon in your gloved hand. Dip the bowl of the spoon into the hot water and immediately press it against the block of dry ice. You'll hear a loud screech.

Dip and press again—but less hard this time. Is the sound louder or softer than before? Dip and press again, rolling the bowl of the spoon against the ice this time. How does this affect the sound. Try different pressing techniques and different spoons. Experiment to see how many different, ghostly tones you can produce. Just be sure to dip before each test because the spoon must be warm to be noisy.

Wondering what's happening to produce these sounds? Dry ice—frozen carbon dioxide—is not only much colder than regular ice, it also melts at a much lower temperature. And when it melts, it changes directly to a gas. This process of changing from a solid to a gas is called sublimation. Metal is a good conductor of heat energy. When you press the spoon against the ice block, heat flows into the dry ice, making it sublimate even faster. The gas that is produced pushes outward, trying to push the spoon away while the person holding the spoon pushes it down. These two opposing forces make the metal vibrate. And these vibrations make the air vibrate, creating sounds—eerie, spooky sounds.

Stir Up a Witch's Brew

NOW, CREATE a special effect that turns plain water into a mysterious brew. Have your adult partner transfer a chunk of the dry ice from the cooler to a Pyrex glass baking dish. Pour on a glassful of warm water and watch what happens.

The warm water raises the temperature of the solid dry ice, causing a lot of it to sublimate suddenly. If the water is deep enough to cover the dry ice, it will appear to boil as the released carbon-dioxide gas bubbles up through it. A thick white cloud also forms on the surface of the water. This cloud isn't the carbon dioxide gas. Like real fog, this is water vapor from the air that was chilled enough to make it condense. Also like real fog, this cloud is denser or heavier than the surrounding air. This makes the fog appear to stay in the dish, floating just above the surface of the water, until enough builds up to spill over.

You can't usually see air currents, but you can observe their movement by watching what they do to the fog. Create some wind by blowing gently into the dish. How does the fog respond to the moving air?

Cause a Spooky Arm Lift

TELL YOUR friends that you can cast a spell that will make a person's arms lift upon your command. Call for a volunteer to help you demonstrate your "powers." Have that person stand in a doorway, arms down, with palms against the door frame. Next, tell your volunteer to press outward and upward as hard as possible—and keep pressing hard—while you say some "magic" words. Say anything you like and count to twenty. Then tell your subject to step forward out of the doorway. Issue a command for your friends arms to rise.

To your subject's amazement, their arms will drift up a little way all by themselves, seeming to follow your command. What really happens is that the person's muscles, after responding to the intense and steady pressure, keep on responding. While this muscular reaction only lasts a few seconds, it's long enough to create an eerie special effect.

Of course Halloween isn't the only special event that happens in autumn. You'll find out about Columbus Day, Diwali, Rosh Hashanah, electing U.S. presidents, and more in the next chapter. So read on.

4.
MORE
SEASONAL
ACTION

Rosh Hashanah

THE JEWISH holiday Rosh Hashanah marks the end of the year's work in the fields and the beginning of a new year, so it is celebrated in the fall. Although it's always on the first day of the Hebrew month of Tishri, the exact date varies from September to early October on the English calendar. This variation occurs because the English calendar is based on the sun and the Hebrew calendar is based on the moon. Rosh Hashanah is always on a new moon.

For this holiday, people share round loaves of bread to show that the seasons go around and that it is once again the New Year. They also eat slices of apple dipped in honey, saying: "May God grant us a good, sweet year."

Besides being a time to celebrate, Rosh Hashanah is a time for prayer and repentance. According to tradition, at this time God opens the books of deeds for the past year. The names of all those who were truly good all year are written in the Book of Life and the names of those who behaved wickedly are written in the Book of Death. Judgment on all those who don't fit into either of these two categories is left suspended until Yom Kippur, ten days later. So the Jewish New Year is a time to be sorry for having sinned and to try to make up for those sins.

Jews spend Yom Kippur in the temple, fasting and praying for forgiveness. With the final service, worshipers make their peace with God. The books of deeds are considered closed and not to be reopened for another year.

Columbus Day

IF YOU'RE in New York City on the second Monday in October, you won't want to miss the big parade up Fifth Avenue. This parade honors Christopher Columbus's discovery of the New World. Columbus actually made four voyages to the New World, exploring new places each time, but his first trip was the hardest and required the most courage.

Imagine leaving home on a small boat not knowing what lies ahead of you, or even if you'll ever return. To get a crew to sign up for such a voyage, royal orders promised a pardon to anyone who would sail with Columbus, so some of the sailors were criminals, trying to stay out of jail. Most, though, were experienced seamen who were seeking fame and fortune. A reward was promised to the first person to spot land, and all who went were promised a share of the fortune they expected to find. Everyone believed that if Columbus did succeed, he and his crew would eventually reach China. And thanks to the travels of an earlier explorer, Marco Polo, everyone knew of China's great wealth of precious gems, beautiful silks, and all sorts of valuable spices.

Actually, Columbus should be remembered as much for sticking with his beliefs as for what he finally accomplished. It took years of effort to finally convince someone who could afford to back him to sponsor this voyage. Columbus began in Portugal, presenting his plans to King John II, who was financing exploration of the African coast. John II considered the venture for a whole year before finally saying no. Columbus then turned to Ferdinand and Isabella, rulers of Spain. They were interested, but too involved in a war to make a commitment. So Isabella appointed a commission to study the project. Months and then years passed. Columbus tried again for Portugal's support, then England's, and France's. No one was interested, and then finally—after seven years of trying—Spain won the war and agreed to sponsor Columbus's expedition.

But the struggle wasn't over. Once at sea, Columbus had to be more strongwilled than ever. Aboard small ships with only ocean and sky as far as they could see, his crew became fearful and discouraged. To make matters worse, after a while the wind ceased to blow them along, their drinking water became stale, and their food rotted or became infested with insects. By the end of September, the men were threatening to take control of the ship. If they hadn't needed Columbus to navigate, they might have done just that.

Luckily, the wind picked up and the sailors began to see birds— usually a sign that land was nearby. Several times early in October, men cried out: "Land ho!" But these turned out to be false alarms. Finally, early on the morning of October 12, 1492, the weary crew actually did spot a small island. Columbus took a landing party ashore, claiming the land for Spain and naming it San Salvador. Everyone believed they had reached what was called the Indies. They had actually landed on one of the small islands of the Bahamas off the coast of Florida. For two weeks, Columbus sailed, throughout the Caribbean, exploring other islands and looking for gold.

At Haiti, Columbus's own ship was wrecked when it struck a reef in the shallow bay. There the natives told him about a gold mine, so Columbus quickly built a fort from the wrecked ship's timbers, left some of the men to guard the mine, and sailed for Spain.

Columbus was welcomed as a hero when he returned from this first voyage. However, when later voyages didn't return with the great fortunes of gold King Ferdinand and Queen Isabella expected, he fell out of favor. Finally, after his fourth voyage, Columbus retired, and although not poor, he was bitter over what he felt were failures. It wouldn't be until many years after his death that people would appreciate how with great persistence and courage, Columbus led the way to the great period of exploration and discovery.

RIDDLE

Where does Wolfman park his car?
In a barking lot.

Sail Your Own Niña, Pinta, and Santa María

NO ONE knows the exact measurements of Columbus's three ships, the *Niña*, the *Pinta*, and the *Santa María*. They do know that two—the *Pinta* and the *Niña*—were caravels, small, fairly fast ships about seventy feet long. The *Santa María* was a nao, a slightly larger, slower vessel. This was the ship on which Columbus sailed to the New World. He returned aboard the *Niña* after the *Santa María* sank off Haiti.

All three ships were wooden and believed to be square-rigged, meaning that their mainsails were square rather than triangular. This shape of sail helped the ships ride more steadily on the rolling waves.

Your *Niña*, *Pinta*, and *Santa María* will need to be steady sailers too, but their ocean will be a cake pan full of water. To make your ships, you'll need: three Styrofoam or waxed paper cups, modeling clay, three round wooden toothpicks, three 4-inch squares of white construction paper, a ruler, a pencil, and scissors.

First, measure up two inches from the base of each cup and make a mark. Measure and mark several more places around the base. Draw a line connecting these points that encircle the cup. Cut straight down from the rim to this mark and cut, following the line, around the cup.

Next, roll balls of modeling clay about the size of a dime and press one into the center of each cup. Thread a toothpick through each paper square as shown below. These are the masts and sails for your ships. Push the upper and lower edges of the paper together slightly to make the sail billow out. And poke one toothpick mast into each ball of clay so it stands straight up.

Fill a cake pan with water and set your boats afloat. Power each ship by positioning your face directly behind it and blowing gently on the sail. What happens if you blow harder—does the boat go faster or does it sink? What happens to the ship if you blow slightly to the right or left instead of straight at the sail?

Try building other sailing ships by shaping aluminum foil and molding modeling clay. Which ship sails best? Have your friends build ships too. Then float the ships in a miniature ocean, such as a plastic wading pool, and hold races.

Was There Someone Before Columbus?

MANY PEOPLE believe that while Columbus's landing was the first documented, he wasn't the first to discover North America for the European's. Leif Eriksson, a Viking explorer, is thought to have made a number of visits to North America about 500 years before Columbus. He and other Vikings are believed to even have settled briefly on the coast of northern New England just below Canada. This theory is based on a thirteenth century account called the

Greenlander Saga and intensive research that has been done in recent years.

According to the saga story, Leif's exploration of North America was sparked by an even earlier voyage. Another Viking ship sailing from Iceland to Greenland became lost in a thick fog. When the mist finally cleared, the sailors saw land—only it wasn't a familiar coast. This ship didn't land, but the sighting was reported. Word of this new land spread and finally reached Norway and the Viking ruler Eric the Red. In about A.D. 1003, Leif, the ruler's son, set sail from the Greenland colony, searching for this new land.

Leif, the Greenlander Saga reports, found North America. It's believed that he first landed in Canada near Baffin Island. Then he sailed southward, landing near southern Labrador and again in New England, which he named Vinland. Leif and his crew are believed to have spent the winter there before returning to Greenland.

For the next few years following Leif's voyage, the Vikings made numerous voyages and established settlements in Vinland. None of these new colonies is believed to have lasted very long, though. The Native Americans—the Indians—were just too unfriendly.

Eventually, because of changes in the climate, the settlements in Greenland were also abandoned by the Vikings.

Was Leif Eriksson really the first of the Europeans to discover North America? No one knows for sure. Many objects, such as iron boat rivets and part of a spindle, that are known to have been made by Vikings more than a thousand years ago have been found near the northern tip of Newfoundland. An ancient Norwegian coin was also found in Maine. Researchers believe these discoveries are proof that the Vikings were definitely in North America before Columbus.

Fall Festival of Lights

IN INDIA, followers of the Hindu religion celebrate the beginning of their new year at the end of October with a holiday called Diwali or the Festival of Lights. This holiday has its origin in a wonderful love story.

According to the legend, Rama, a brave prince, fought a great battle with a terrible ten-headed, ten-armed demon king named Ravana to rescue his wife, Sita. Then the happy couple began a long journey back to their own land. As word of Rama's success spread, proud and delighted subjects turned out to welcome them. And thousands of small clay lamps called diva were set out along the trail to light the couple's way.

Today at Diwali, Hindu homes in India still glow with lots of small diva set on roofs, in windows, and edging paths to doorways. Now, though, the people do this also because they believe they are lighting the way for Lakshmi, the goddess of prosperity. A brightly lit home has the best chance of receiving the gift of good fortune for the coming year. Women and girls also set clay clamps afloat on lakes and rivers. Any diva that is till glowing when it reaches the opposite shore is supposed to bring good luck to its owner.

Electing a U.S. President

EVERY FOUR years in the fall, citizens of the United States have an opportunity to vote for a new president. This election day, which occurs on the first Tuesday after the first Monday in November, is actually only part of the process that ends with the president taking office.

Months earlier, the people who want to become president begin to try to win public support. Their first goal is to become their party's candidate. Currently, there are only two main parties in the United States: the Democratic party and the Republican party. To get the list of people from which voters have to choose down to two—one from each party—primary elections are held in each state. The date for these elections varies from state to state. In recent presidential election years, though, a large number of states held their primaries on the same day so that this event came to be known as "Super Tuesday." What people are really selecting at the primary are representatives to attend the party's national convention.

At the party convention, two important things happen. First, the representatives work to develop their platform, the principles for which the party will stand and the issues it will support. Next, the representatives vote to select one person to become their presidential candidate. Then the candidate also selects the person who will run for the vice presidential position. While this person's job is much less important than the president's, on a number of

occasions, the president has died, been killed, or resigned. Then the vice president has had to assume the role of president, so it's critical that this person be capable of handling that job.

The right to vote for president has greatly expanded over the years. At first, only white, male, landowners could vote. In Massachusetts you also had to be an active member of the Congregational Church. A poll tax or fee and literacy tests were also used to limit who could vote in different states. Blacks were granted the right to vote in 1870, but it took nearly another hundred years to eliminate the many barriers, to this right. Women finally received the vote in 1920, after years of struggling for it. And in 1971, the voting age was lowered from twenty-one to eighteen, extending the right to vote to those who were being drafted into the army to fight for their country.

What many people don't realize is that when they vote on election day, they aren't really voting for a presidential candidate. They're selecting electors from their state. Each state has a number of electors—the same number as the combined total of the state's congressional representatives and senators. Some states like California and New York have many electoral votes and others such as Alaska and Wyoming have only a few. On election day, the candidate receiving the greatest number of votes in a state receives that state's electoral votes.

In December, the states' electoral votes are counted and the candidate receiving the majority wins. If no candidate receives a majority, the House of Representatives chooses the president from whatever three candidates had the most electoral votes. The election decision has gone to the House on several occasions—sometimes with startling results. Rutherford B. Hayes, for example, received fewer popular votes than his opponent, Samuel Tilden, but was tied for electoral votes. The vote in the House finally established Hayes as the winner.

On January 20, the winning candidate takes the oath of office and becomes president of the United States. The job of chief executive is a big one. The president makes sure all federal laws are enforced, encourages Congress to pass new laws to support his party's platform, and can veto or kill a law unless Congress repasses the law with two-thirds of the representatives supporting it. The president is also the commander in chief of all the armed services and acting in this position speaks for the United States when dealing with all foreign nations.

Being president is hard work, but it is also very rewarding to be able to do so much for your country. You may one day want to run for this job. To be eligible, you only need to meet these qualifications: be a U.S. citizen from birth; be at least thirty-five years old; and have been a resident of the United States for the past fourteen years.

If you did decide to run for president, what would you do to encourage people to vote for you? If you were elected, what would you want to change about the United States? What would you most want to prevent from changing?

RIDDLE

What kind of horses do ghosts and goblins ride?
Nightmares.

A Little Party History

THERE WEREN'T any political parties when George Washington became president. A difference in opinion soon developed between two of Washington's aides, Alexander Hamilton and Thomas Jefferson, over many issues. The basic difference, however, was that Hamilton favored an aristocratic government that supported the rich. Jefferson, on the other hand, was passionately concerned with securing equal rights and representation for everyone. Hamilton's supporters became the Federalist party and those who shared Jefferson's views became the Democratic-Republican party. Later they were known only as the Democrats. The donkey became the symbol for this party in 1828, when Andrew Jackson used it as a symbol after being called a "jackass" by his opponents.

Later, another party gained strength to oppose the Democrats. Members of this party called themselves Whigs after the Whig party that was active in England. Like the Federalists of the early days, the Whigs favored the elite of society. Mostly, though, they were a party made up of many smaller opposition groups. They had trouble uniting behind a candidate until they chose to run General William Henry Harrison, who was a famous Indian fighter. Harrison was elected, but died from pneumonia, after only thirty-two days in office. Later, they were able to elect a second hero, General Zachery Taylor. He, unfortunately, collapsed from sunstroke and died only sixteen months after taking office.

Without Taylor as a rallying point, the Whigs once more broke up into groups supporting specific issues. In the 1850s, there were suddenly a whole group of political parties—the strongest was the Know-Nothings, a party based on the hatred of immigrants and Catholics.

The Republican party finally emerged in 1854 as a party of the north, supporting the workingman and against slavery. In 1860,

Cartoonist Thomas Nast established the donkey as the symbol of the Democratic party and the elephant as the symbol of the Republican party in the late 1800s.

Abraham Lincoln became the first Republican to be elected president. For the next fifty years–except for Grover Cleveland—a Republican would be president. It was during this time that the party became known as the GOP, the Grand Old Party. And a political cartoonist was the first to use the elephant as the party's symbol.

Democrat Woodrow Wilson stopped the Republicans' chain of victories in 1912. Since that time, control has passed back and forth between the Democrats and the Republicans. Franklin D. Roosevelt, a Democrat, was the only president to hold office for more than two terms. An amendment to the Constitution now makes it impossible for anyone to be elected more than twice. During all this time, additional smaller parties have developed and died only to be replaced by others. These groups continue to play an important role by providing an opportunity for people with different views to work together to have their opinions heard.

Presidential Stumpers

HOW WELL do you know the past presidents of the United States? Number from one to twenty on a piece of paper. Then take this quiz to test yourself, writing the answer next to each number. The names of all the presidents are listed in the next section. You won't use all of the presidents, though, and you may use some more than once. Finally, look at the answers on page 00. Visit the library and check in books and encyclopedias to find out more about the presidents.

1. Which president was the first to live in the White House?
2. Who was the only son of a president to become president?
3. Who was the youngest president?
4. Who was the first president to have a beard?
5. Which president had the most children?
6. Who was the only president to be elected by unanimous vote, meaning that absolutely everyone who voted voted for him?
7. Who was president for only one month?
8. Which president resigned from office?
9. Which president was never married?
10. Who was the oldest president ever to be elected?
11. Who was the only president ever to be elected to four terms?
12. Which president was the first to toss out a baseball at the opening of baseball season?
13. Who was the first vice president to become president on the death of a president?

14. Who was president when the White House got the first bathtub with running water?
15. Who was the only president born on the Fourth of July?
16. Who is the only president to have also served as chief justice of the Supreme Court?
17. Which president was the heaviest?
18. Who was the first vice president to advance to the position of president without having been elected by the people.
19. Who was president when the telephone was installed at the White House?
20. Who were the tallest and shortest presidents?

Presidents of the United States

George Washington
   1789–1797
John Adams 1797–1801
Thomas Jefferson
   1801–1809
James Madison 1809–1817
James Monroe 1817–1825
John Quincy Adams
   1825–1829
Andrew Jackson
   1829–1837
Martin Van Buren
   1837–1841

William Henry Harrison
   1841–1841
John Tyler 1841–1845
James Knox Polk
   1845–1849
Zachary Taylor 1849–1850
Millard Fillmore 1850–1853
Franklin Pierce 1853–1857
James Buchanan
   1857–1861
Abraham Lincoln
   1861–1865
Andrew Johnson 1865–1969

Ulysses Simpson Grant
1869–1877
Rutherford Birchard Hayes
1877–1881
James Abram Garfield
1881–1881
Chester Alan Arthur
1881–1885
Grover Cleveland 1885–1889;
1893–1897
Benjamin Harrison
1889–1893
William McKinley 1897–1901
Theodore Roosevelt
1901–1909
William Howard Taft
1909–1913
Woodrow Wilson 1913–1921
Warren Gamaliel Harding
1921–1923

Calvin Coolidge 1923–1929
Herbert Clark Hoover
1929–1933
Franklin Delano Roosevelt
1933–1945
Harry S. Truman 1945–1953
Dwight David Eisenhower
1953–1961
John Fitzgerald Kennedy
1961–1963
Lyndon Baines Johnson
1963–1969
Richard Milhous Nixon
1969–1974
Gerald Rudolph Ford
1974–1977
James Earl Carter 1977–1981
Ronald Reagan 1981–1989
George Herbert Walker Bush
1989–

It Can't Be Right!

THAT'S WHAT the CBS news crew said about the UNIVAC I computer on election night, November 4, 1952. For the first time in history a computer was being used to predict the outcome of a presidential election. The computer had done its job, but nobody believed it could have worked correctly. With only three million votes counted, a mere five percent of the total, the computer had analyzed the results and predicted that Dwight Eisenhower would win by a landslide. Landslide victories are rare in presidential elections, and CBS officials were reluctant to make such a prediction based on so few votes—and the opinion of a computer.

People were not used to working with computers in the early 1950s, and, in fact, UNIVAC I was very different from today's computers. For one thing it was huge, occupying nearly 1,200 square feet and weighing about 30,000 pounds. It's memory consisted of 5,000 big glass tubes that looked something like oddly shaped light bulbs switched on and off as they processed and stored information.

To prepare UNIVAC I for the big job of analyzing election data, programmers listened to recordings of hour-by-hour radio broadcasts of previous presidential-election nights. From these, they developed a pattern of what had happened in various parts of the country in the past. Then they wrote a program for the computer that would simulate that same kind of voting behavior based on any current results.

CBS finally announced that the computer predicted that Eisenhower would win, but they didn't add "by a landslide." Later, when this indeed proved to be true, reporters admitted what had happened. They explained that the computer had been right, but that no one had believed it. How different from the present when television news reports depend on computers to make a quick prediction of the winner—sometimes even before the polls have closed on the West Coast of the United States.

Answers to Presidential Stumpers

1. John Adams moved into the White House when only six rooms were finished. Mrs. Adams hung the family's wash in the East Room.
2. John Quincy Adams.
3. Theodore Roosevelt, who was only forty-two when President William McKinley was assassinated and he became president.
4. Abraham Lincoln.
5. John Tyler was the father of fifteen children.
6. George Washington.
7. William Henry Harrison caught a cold on inauguration day. He soon developed pneumonia and died.
8. Richard Nixon resigned in 1974 after seven former aides were indicted for trying to install wiretapping devices in the headquarters of the National Democratic Committee in the Watergate building in Washington, D.C.
9. James Buchanan.
10. Ronald Reagan was sixty-nine at the time of his election.
11. Franklin Delano Roosevelt was, but he died in office while serving his fourth term.
12. William Howard Taft started that tradition in 1910.
13. John Tyler was the first, assuming the presidency when William Henry Harrison died.
14. Millard Fillmore.

15. Calvin Collidge.

16. William Howard Taft was president from 1909 to 1913. Then in 1921, President Harding appointed him chief justice.

17. William Howard Taft weighed about three hundred pounds.

18. Gerald Rudolph Ford was chosen by President Richard Nixon to become vice president in 1973 when Spiro Agnew had to resign this position. In 1974, when Nixon resigned, Ford became president.

19. Rutherford B. Hayes was, and he even got a demonstration of how to use it from Alexander Graham Bell, the telephone's inventor.

20. Many of the presidents have been tall, but Abraham Lincoln was the tallest—six feet, four inches. James Madison was shortest—five feet, four inches.

RIDDLE

What kind of boats do vampires own?

Blood vessels.

A Tropical Terror

ALTHOUGH HURRICANE season starts in June, it continues through November. Hurricanes (called typhoons in the western Pacific and China Sea) are the largest storms in the world. They are often hundreds of miles wide, travel thousands of miles, and rage on with deadly force for more than a week before finally fading away.

Hurricanes generally originate near the equator, where the sun heats the ocean, causing the water to evaporate quickly. The faster this happens the stronger the upward surging current of air becomes. This causes surrounding warm air to rush in, replacing the rapidly rising air. The effect is like a pump. Thunderstorm clouds form, and the earth's natural rotation is enough to start these storm clouds spinning, cycling.

Satellite photos provide a vividly clear picture of the spiraling clouds. When the winds reach thirty-nine miles per hour, the storm system is classified as a tropical storm. If the pumping action continues to speed the winds up to seventy-four miles per hour, the storm officially becomes a hurricane. Some hurricane winds have been recorded blowing as strongly as two hundred miles per hour. At the very center of the storm spiral, there is an area of relative calm, the hurricane's eye.

In addition to wind damage, hurricanes have other destructive forces. Hurricanes produce heavy rains and a sea surge, high waves created by the storm's strong winds. If a sea surge is coupled with high tide, a massive wall of water may push ashore.

Hurricanes were first named in Puerto Rico, where they were given the name of the saint's day when they struck land. After World War II, men who forecast the weather began naming these powerful storms after their wives or girlfriends. To be fair, hurricanes are now named according to an official list selected for each year. This list contains male names as well as female names.

While hurricanes still cause tremendous damage, they no longer claim as many lives. Satellite photos allow meteorologists, people who study the weather, to track the storm's path and predict where it is likely to strike land. Then the weather people will know what city or cities need to be evacuated to protect its citizens from this terrible storm.

Because it's such a relief each year when hurricane season is over the Virgin Islands celebrates this event on the third Monday in October.

Do you know what color scarlet tanagers and weasels become in the fall? Or how honeybees prepare their hives for winter? Could you identify the kind of birds flocking past overhead just by their flight pattern? You'll learn the answers in the next chapter. And you'll discover a lot more about what animals do in autumn—next.

5.
ANIMALS IN AUTUMN

A Fall Song

AUTUMN IS a season of change for many animals. For some, it's the season to find a mate. That's why crickets and grasshoppers "sing." These insects only produce their tunes when they reach sexual maturity, and that happens in the fall. It's also only the males that make sounds, trying to attract any listening females.

These insect musicians create their tunes by rubbing one body part against another so it's really more like playing an instrument than singing. Grasshoppers rub their enlarged hind legs—first one and then the other in turn—against the edges of their forewings. Crickets rub one leg over the other. Crickets have tightly stretched membranes on their wings that act as sound amplifiers.

Chirping can be dangerous for these insect suitors, though, because the songs are likely to attract enemies as well as mates. Birds, frogs, toads, and even parasitic flies are able to locate the male crickets and grasshoppers by following the sounds they make.

Cricket

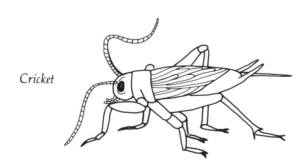

Dressed for Success

FALL IS the mating season for elk too, and each year the males or bulls, grow antlers just for this event. Antlers are made of bone, and during most of the time that the male elk have this impressive crown they've covered with a velvety-soft layer of skin. The antlers sprout each year in the spring and then grow rapidly. Young yearling bulls have only a single swordlike spike. Older bulls have broadly spreading antlers with many branches. Such large headgear is heavy, but it does have one advantage. Blood flowing through the skin covering the antlers radiates away body heat. So the bigger the antlers, the more effective this built-in cooling system on a hot summer day.

As autumn approaches, blood stops flowing to the skin coating the antlers. Then this sheath begins to peel like sunburned skin. The bulls rub against saplings and shrubs to help remove the irritating flaking skin. Finally, only the hard bony antlers remain.

Antlers

Antlers are definitely power dressing. The bigger a bull's headgear the more females or cows he attracts for his herd. A large antler display also makes it easier for him to keep his herd. If another bull approaches, the two meet in antler-to-antler combat. The battle is almost always brief, though, and seldom ends in serious injury, because the elk with the biggest antlers is recognized as being superior. So the bull with the less impressive headgear quickly yields.

During the winter, the males shed their antlers, dropping them in the snow. Then, come spring, the process begins again. A year older, the bulls sprout an even bigger and more impressive set of antlers in preparation for the fall mating season.

Pretty Foxy

LATE AUTUMN is also the breeding season for red foxes, and two males will fight for possession of a mate. The conflict begins with the two males circling each other, their fur bristling. If possible, one male will flip its bushy tail into the other's face. In that instant while it's opponent's vision is blocked, the male with the sudden advantage will charge, knocking the other male off his feet. If one

male is unable to outfox the other in this way, the two are likely to rear up on their hind feet. Then they lash out with their front feet and bite whenever they have the opportunity. Despite the fierceness of the battle, the weaker male seems to know when to quit, so the loser is seldom seriously injured. The victor doesn't pursue the fight, being satisfied to have won the female of his choice.

The Truth about Ants in Autumn

ACCORDING TO some fables, ants are especially active in the fall because they're storing food for the cold winter months ahead. It is true that ants are more active than ever during this season. Many plants have gone to seed, and harvester ants, for example, are at their busiest, collecting and storing seeds. The aphid population is also at its peak at this time of year. So the aphid-tending ants are busier than ever too. They must constantly carry their charges from plant to plant so the aphids can suck the plant's juices and produce a supply of honeydew for the ants. Scientists who study ants report, however, that none of this fall activity is done to get ready for winter.

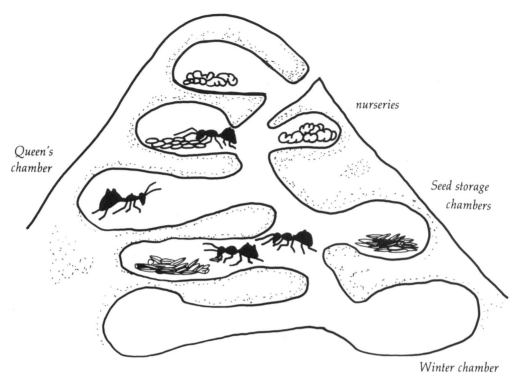

Queen's chamber

nurseries

Seed storage chambers

Winter chamber

In parts of the world where winters are cold, ants prepare for this season by digging their tunnels deeper—deep enough to be below the frost line, the depth to which the ground usually freezes. Then they spend the cold wintertime huddled together hibernating. When an animal hibernates, its body processes are so slowed that it doesn't need to eat. So the food the ant colony stockpiles isn't their winter supply. Instead, scientists believe that all this harvesting is done to prepare the ant colony for periods of drought or prolonged periods of rain during their active spring and summer months.

For many ant colonies, autumn is also the mating season. Winged males and female "queens" are produced at this time. After a mating flight, the males die and each queen digs a shallow burrow and seals herself inside. There, safe and snug, the queen hibernates throughout the winter. In the spring, she will begin a new colony.

On the Ant Trail

BECAUSE ANTS are so active in the fall, it's a good time to observe their behavior. Take a notebook with you so you can keep a journal of your ant safari. Describe the ants you find and where you obeserve them. Then answer these questions as you watch the ants in action:

1.   About how far does does one ant travel in a minute?
2.   Do the ants appear to be following a trail?
3.   If any ant is carrying something, how big is its burden compared to its body size?
4.   How does the ant carry its load?
5.   What does an ant do when it comes to an obstacle such as a twig or stone in its path? (If there isn't any obstacle in sight, place one in the ant's path.)

For more action, take along some sugar in a self-sealing plastic sandwhich bag. When you spot some ants, put a pinch of sugar on the ground near the ants. Then observe how the ants react. Write everything you observe in your journal.

When the ants discover the sugar, do other ants arrive soon after, marching in line as though following a trail? When ants discover a new food supply, they quickly return to their nest, creating an odor trail for other ants to follow. To do this, the ants release droplets of special chemicals called pheromones from glands in their abdomen. Sensitive hairs on the ants' feelers or antennae let them recognize trails made by members of their own colony even when they cross those made by ants from other colonies. Unless constantly reinforced, though, the odor trails quickly fade. This keeps ants from traveling a trail that has no reward at the end and protects the ants from enemies that have an equally good sense of smell.

When there is a break in the line of ants, draw your finger across the path. Can new ants coming along the trail still find their way to the sugar? Or has your odor destroyed the scent trail?

Autumn Travelers

AUTUMN IS a season when many animals are on the move. Some travel from places where winters are usually very cold and food is likely to be scarce to warmer regions sure to have a plentiful food supply. Others travel to traditional breeding grounds in order to find a mate and reproduce. How do these animals know when to begin their journey, find their way along a precise route—often one they have never traveled before—and go to the same location their kind has moved to for all time? Those are the great mysteries of animal behavior, which scientists are still investigating and trying to understand. Here's a closer look at some fall travelers.

Canada Geese

IN LATE October, flocks of Canada geese, often made up of hundreds of birds, begin to move southward. No one is sure what triggers their departure, but as the birds rise higher they begin to move into a pattern. Slowly, this pattern assumes a loose V-outline with the birds flapping close together as though part of a well-organized air force.

Canada Geese

Higher and higher the flock soars, normally leveling out at about 3,000 feet but sometimes flying as high as 9,000 feet. At the point of this V-formation there is just one bird—the leader. While scientists don't completely understand why the geese follow this formation, it's believed that the leader is an especially strong bird. As the leader flies, its wings create updrafts. The birds following stay slightly to the outside of the bird ahead of them. In this way, all but the lead bird are able to take advantage of the updrafts created by the flapping of the other birds' wings. This makes for easier flying and lets the flock keep going for a much longer time. This slightly offset positioning also lets each bird in the V-pattern have a clear view of the sky ahead. The leaders change off frequently so that no one bird has to make the supreme effort for very long.

Watch for these birds in the fall. If you spot a flock of geese, observe it carefully to answer these questions:

1. How wide a V is the flock's formation? How many birds are in the V?

2.   Are the sides of the V straight or wavy?
3.   Do the same birds always seems to maintain the same position within the V-formation or do they move around?
4.   What happens to birds that lag behind?
5.   Does the flock appear to be crossing the sky quickly or slowly?

Canadian geese usually fly about forty miles per hour. To escape a storm or if there is a tail wind, flocks have been clocked flying at more than sixty miles per hour.

Listen for the sounds the geese make too. The birds within the flock constantly call to each other—kind of like a buddy system—to help keep track of each other without looking around. Some say the sounds are like honking or barking. Others think the sounds are like screams. How would you describe the geese calls?

The geese flock may fly for about twelve hours nonstop. Then the birds will find a spot to rest for several days. Horcion Marsh in east-central Wisconsin is a National Wildlife Refuge where the migrating geese stop annually, safe from hunters. Flying and resting, the flock gradually makes its way southward to its wintering grounds in the region where the Ohio River joins the Mississippi River.

Other Flocks to Watch For

THE MAJORITY of birds migrating in large flocks don't follow any definite group flight pattern. So what appears to be a whole cloud of birds could be a flock of starlings, swallows, or any of a number of others. Besides geese, pelicans and golden plovers fly in V-formations. Cranes often fly single file.

Geese

Some birds, such as plovers, seem to move with a sort of synchronization. So even during a sudden change in direction, the whole flock moves together, maintaining its compact formation.

You may also see or hear the cries of migrating flocks if you're outdoors on a moonlight autumn night. Warblers, thrushes, and robins are among the birds that travel at night. Swallows, hawks and other birds of prey, and purple martins are birds you'll spot on the move during the day.

Where Are They Going?

IF YOU live where birds are leaving in autumn, you've probably wondered where they're heading. Here are the destinations of a few common North American birds:

Birds	Destination
Robins	Southern states along both coasts and into Mexico
House wrens	Mexico
Ruby-throated hummingbirds	Central America
Purple Martins	From southern Florida and Mexico southward to Brazil
Barn swallows	From California and the southern states throughout Mexico, Honduras, and Cuba
Red-winged blackbirds	Coastal southern states and Mexico

Bison

THE LARGEST land mammal in North America is the American buffalo or bison. Males weigh as much as a ton. Before the late 1800s, when there were large areas of open prairie and huge herds containing millions of animals, the bison moved seasonally between their grazing ranges. All summer the herds grazed on the grasslands of the northern states. But in the autumn, as heat and

drought dried up this food supply, the herds moved south. Accounts say that the traveling buffalo herds sometimes moved in a single huge column measuring up to fifty miles wide and other times in several parallel columns. The regular trails they followed were so well beaten that surveyors followed them when planning the rail lines. And that changed everything for the migrating herds.

Between 1870 and 1875, hunters with newly improved, quick-loading rifles—many of them working for the railroads—killed so many buffalo that by 1889 only 540 remained. Today, through careful protection, that number has increased to around 20,000 animals. But these buffalo live on game reserves, national parks, and private farms. The herds no longer follow their traditional seasonal treks across the North American prairies.

Eels

IN THE fall they become full grown (about four years for males and from seven to twelve years for females), European eels stop feeding and go through a remarkable change. Their normal skin color of yellowish gray changes to olive green or dark brown with a silvery-white belly. Their head becomes more pointed and their eyes become much larger than normal. Then the eels begin to migrate. The females, which have lived in freshwater rivers up until this time, first swim to the coast where the males live. Then the adults head out into the Atlantic.

Meanwhile American eels go through a similar change, migrate to the East Coast of the United States, and head out to sea. Although the two groups carry on separate life cycles, they both travel long distances to reach the same place in the ocean. This spot, called the Sargasso Sea, is a deep area in the middle of the Atlantic where thick brown seaweed floats over the surface. The trip takes all winter, and shortly after they arrive, the adults mate, lay their eggs, and die.

The young eels, which are only a quarter of an inch long, transparent, and shaped like willow leaves, hatch and remain in the seaweed, feeding on plankton and microscopic plant and animal life floating in the ocean. Gradually—although no one yet understands how they know where to go—the European eel youngsters head for Europe and the American eel youngsters head for North America. Too small to swim at this time, the baby eels drift in the ocean currents. It takes as long as three years for the young eels to reach Europe, but only a year for the American eels to reach the coast.

Finally, those that survive this long journey reach the mouths of the rivers where their mothers lived years earlier. The males remain along the coast and the females swim upstream to live and grow until one fall when they reach maturity and the cycle will be complete once again.

Traveling Fish

A NUMBER of different kinds of fish that live in large groups or schools are on the move in the fall. For example, smelt, which in the summer live in the cool deeper waters of the Atlantic, move into tidal bays. They remain there until spring, when they move upstream to spawn—lay their eggs.

Herring migrations are so regular that they're counted on by the fishing industry in Britain and northwestern Europe. From September into December, large schools of these fish, often called herring shoals, can be counted on off eastern Scottish ports and later off northeastern English ports.

Why do the herring make this annual trip? Scientists have discovered that the herring come into shallow water to spawn. Their eggs, unlike most fish eggs, which float, are heavier than seawater and are deposited in crevices on the stony sea bottom in shallow water. This provides the herring eggs with more protection than those that drift on the surface. Another fish, called the pilchard, also comes close to shore in the fall to spawn. The young of these fish are caught and canned as the popular food sardines.

Big schools of mackerel are also known to migrate in the fall, but these fish don't travel closer to shore. Instead, unlike most fish, they travel away from shore and swim down, down, down to much deeper-than-usual ocean ranges. Fishing trawlers rarely catch mackerel during the winter because they remain at such depths.

New Fall Coats

FOR SOME animals, fall is a season to change color. Some male birds who wear bright colors to attract a mate during the spring and summer change to camouflage coloring that will match the southern forests toward which they'll be heading in the fall. Male goldfinches change their bright yellow plummage for the same drab olive brown the females wear. Male bobolinks also change in the fall so that their coloring matches their mates' olive and black. And scarlet tanager males go from bright red to olive green.

Both male and female ptarmagans also change to camouflage coloring in the fall. But because these birds live where the ground is snow-covered throughout much of the winter, they change from reddish brown to snowy white.

A weasel's brown fur coat turns white in the fall too. This process begins in the middle of October with the fur close to the animal's nose and proceeds gradually toward its tail. About two months later, the change is complete and the weasel is white except for the black tip of its tail. This furry tip, which is about an inch and a half long, is a trick. Although now camouflaged, the weasel's movements may still attract an enemy, such as a bird of prey. This enemy will most likely dive at what it can see best, though. So the most visible part of the weasel is its tail tip, the least vulnerable part of its body.

Unfortunately for the weasel, its black tail doesn't fool its worst enemy—people. In fact, this black-tipped tail and white fur are considered especially attractive. The weasel's winter fur, called ermine, has been used for centuries as trim for an Indian chief's warbonnet, the edging of a king's royal robe, and even for fur coats.

Fall's Feast

A number of animals store the fall harvest by eating a lot and developing layers of fat. This fat can later be broken down by the body to produce energy for body activities and warmth.

Bears are famous for stuffing themselves year round, but they really gain weight in the fall when food is plentiful. In fact, studies have shown that they often gain more than two hundred pounds between August and October.

Raccoons also have tremendous appetites during this season. If enough wild foods aren't available to satisfy them, suburban raccoons will eat the seeds out of bird feeders and raid garbage cans.

Badgers are big fall eaters too. They prefer meat, such as mice, gophers, rabbits, and earthworms. However, in the fall, they're also happy to dine on roots, grasses, and berries. Since they are naturally nocturnal, or active at night, fall's longer nights allow badgers extra eating time. Badgers often get so chubby in the fall that they can barely walk to their next dining site.

Besides the fact that food is plentiful, bears, raccoons, and badgers eat heartily in the fall to prepare for winter. Although not true hibernators, these animals stay snuggled inside dens and sleep during cold weather. Then with their body temperature lower than normal and their heart and breathing rate slower than normal, the fat reserves they built up in autumn are enough to keep their bodies fueled.

RIDDLE

What do ghosts chew?
Boobble gum.

Storing It Away

Some animals take advantage of the fall harvest to build up a food stash for winter when food will be in short supply. Acorn woodpeckers of the west and southwest are appropriately named because they store acorns. The bird makes an acorn-sized hole in a tree trunk or fence post by drilling at high speed with its sharp beak. Then it carries a single nut to this hole and pokes it in. Each acorn is stored in a separately drilled hole.

Female mud-dauber wasps store food too, but this food supply is for their developing young. In autumn, the female wasps build nests under eaves or tucked in other sheltered spots by using mud 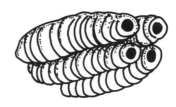 to fashion many small cells like little pots stacked one above the other.

As each cell is completed, she hunts for a spider, stings it to paralyze but not kill it, and carries it back to the nest. Next, she tucks the spider inside and lays an egg on top of it. The wasp continues adding onto and stocking her nursery until she has laid about a dozen eggs. Then she seals the opening of the nest with more mud. Even more mud may be smeared on the outside of the now vaselike nest. When it hardens, this will be a safe, snug winter home. And after they hatch, the grublike larva or young will be able to feed all winter on the stored food.

Getting Their Houses Ready for Winter

For animals, like people in parts of the world where the winter is likely to be cold, fall is the season for weatherproofing their homes. Honeybees collect sticky gum from buds and trees. Then the workers use this to seal cracks in the walls of their wax hive. Badgers and skunks carry loads of dead grass and leaves into their dens to insulate them from the cold.

Jumping mice, distant cousins of the gerbils people sometimes keep as pets, dig special winter homes. First, the mouse digs down deeper than the ground is likely to freeze during the winter. Next, it prepares a nest of dried grass and leaves and plugs the tunnel entrance. Snug behind its closed door, the mouse curls up in a small furry ball to hibernate during the cold weather ahead.

Even though it has a built-in house, a snail still winterizes its home in the fall. After crawling under a log or other shelter, the snail produces a cementlike material to seal the opening of its shell. Like the jumping mouse, the snail hibernates—safe inside—until spring.

Winter Sleepers

Some animals, such as snails, jumping mice, earthworms, and spiders, settle down in the fall for what will be a very long sleep, lasting the whole winter season ahead. This long sleep is called hibernation, and it's different from just going to sleep at night. When an animal hibernates, its breathing rate slows to only once or twice a minute and its heart rate similarly slows to as few as five beats per minute. The animals body temperature also drops greatly. With so little body activity, the animal's supply of fat fuel is consumed very, very slowly. By the end of the winter, though, all of the bulk stored up in the fall will be gone. A ground squirrel, for example, usually loses about eighty percent of its body weight while hibernating.

While most butterflies are in the pupa stage in the fall and spend the winter safely inside a cocoon, some butterflies also hibernate. The mourning cloak adult, for example, crawls under a bit of bark or a piece of loose siding on a house for its long sleep.

Baby orb-web weaver spiders hibernate in the special egg case their mothers spin for them. In the fall, the orb-web weavers mate. Then in a sheltered spot under a twig, some bark, or other safe spot, the female lays her eggs in a silken sac that is surrounded by an insulating layer of matted silk and covered all over by a parchment like coating to protect it from the cold. Inside, the young spiders hatch and eat their eggshell. Some even eat a few of the other spiders. Those that remain hibernate until spring.

In the fall, the old wasp queen and all the workers who served her throughout the summer die. The new young queens and males that are left mate and then the males die. Each of the queens finds a sheltered spot under an eave or in a hollow tree and hibernates until spring, when they begin to raise the first members of their new colony.

Raccoons, like bears and skunks, are animals that don't hibernate, but they do go to sleep when the weather turns cold. Finding a den in a sheltered spot, such as a tree hollow, several adult raccoons may even snooze down together. When the weather improves, they wake up and go searching for food and water.

The End (for This Year)

Once the first hard frost spreads its shimmering ice coating across yards and meadows and the last colorful leaves have drifted down, autumn is over. Oh, a last straggling flock or two of birds may still pass overhead. And the squirrels may continue scampering up and down tree trunks with nuts in their mouths. Hibernating animals will all have settled down to sleep, though. The wasp's paper house will be empty, and the bees will all remain home in their hive.

Winter will bring a lot of new things for you to do, but autumn exploring—that colorful, mouth-watering, almost magical season of discovery—is over.

You'll have to wait until the next time it's autumn to investigate and find those seasonal wonders again.

INDEX

Acorn woodpeckers 145–146
Adams, John 125
Adams, John Quincy 125
All Saints' Day 67–68
Antlers 131–132
Ants
  food storage 133–134
  trails 135–136
Apples
  bobbing 99–100
  carving a head 29–30
  making sauce 28–29
  planting 30–31
  varieties 26–28
Aster 21
Autumnal equinox 2–3, 5

Badgers 145
Bears 144–145, 148
Bees
  African killer bees 86–87
  honeybees 146–147
Bison (American buffalo) 140–141
Black widow spiders 84–85
Bobolink 143
Bogi 74–75
Bouncing Bet 17
Buchanan, James 125
Buffalo (see *Bison*)

Caesar, Julius 5
Calendar adjustment 5–6
Canada geese 136–139
Carver, George Washington 38
Cattails 47
Celts 66–68, 99
Chapman, John (see *Johnny Appleseed*)

Cleveland, Grover 120
Closed gentian 20–21
Cobras 87–88
Color change 143–144
Columbus, Christopher
  explorations 108–110
  ships 110–111
Columbus Day 108
Constellations
  Andromeda 23–24
  Cassiopeia 23–24
  Cepheus 23–24
  Perseus 23–24
Coolidge, Calvin 125
Corn 31–32, 60
Cornhusk doll 33–37
Cornucopia legend 26
Cotton 39–40
Cranberries 61–63
Cranes 138
Crickets 130

Daylight saving time 3–4
Democratic party 118–122
Diwali 114–115
Druids 66–67

Eriksson, Leif 112–114
Eels 60, 141–142
Elk 131–132
Ermine 144

Federalist party 118–119
Fillmore, Millard 125
Fire ants 85–86
Food chain 12

Ford, Gerald   126
Fossils   98
Frost   7–8

Geranium   50
Goldenrod   18
Goldfinch   143
Golden plovers   138–139
Goober peas (see *Peanuts*)
Great white sharks   83–84

Halloween   66–67
Hamilton, Alexander   118
Harrison, William Henry   119, 125
Harvesting machines   43–44
Haskall, John   43–44
Hawks   139
Hayes, Rutherford B.   126
Herring   143
Hhung-Ch'iu   53–54
Hibernation   147–148
Hopi   70–71
House wrens   140
Hurricanes   126–127

Indian summer   15–16
Investigations
   ant observations   135–136
   apples   28
   arm lift   104–105
   bend a bone   101–102
   boat races   111–112
   cranberry freshness test   62
   dry ice   102–104
   frost   7
   illusions   100–101
   seed parts   50–51
   seed hunt   51–52
Iroquois   70

Jack-o'-lanterns   73–78
Jackson, Andrew   118

Jefferson, Thomas   118
Jewelweed   49–50
Joe-pye weed   19–20
Johnny Appleseed   30–31
Jumping mice   147

Kachinas   71
Know-Nothing party   119
Komodo dragons   92–93
Kwakiutl   70

Leap Year   5
Leap Day   5
Leaves
   buds   11
   collage   13–14
   color change   8–9
   decomposition   12
   printing with   14–15
   scars   11
Lincoln, Abraham   54, 122, 125, 126
Lionfish   82

Mackerel   143
Maize (see *Corn*)
Maple trees   45–46
Masks   69–71
Mayflower   56–57
McCormick, Cyrus   43
Migration   136–143
Mistletoe   46–47
Moore, Hiram   43–44
Mosquitoes   88–89
Muck olla   68

Night vision   93–94
Nixon, Richard   125

Peanuts   37–38
Peanut butter   38
Pelicans   138
Photosynthesis   9

Pilchard   143
Pilgrims   55–59
Pokeweed   22
Political parties (U.S.)   118–120
Pomona   67
Pope Gregory XIII   5–6
Presidential elections (U.S.)   115–126
Ptarmagans   144
Pumpkins
   carving   77–78
   growing   75–77
   seeds   78–79
Purple martins   140

Raccoons   145, 148
Reagan, Ronald   125
Red foxes   132–133
Red-winged blackbirds   140
Republican party   118–122
Robins   139–140
Romans   5, 53, 67, 99
Roosevelt, Franklin Delano   120, 125
Roosevelt, Theodore   125
Rosh Hashanah   107
Ruby-throated hummingbirds   140

Samhain   66–67
Scarecrows   40–42
Scarlet tanager   143
Scorpions   81
Seeds   44–53
Seed mosaic   52–53
Skeletons   94–98
Smelt   142
Snails   147
Squanto   59–61
Sticktights   46
Sukkoth   54

Swallows   139, 140

Taft, William Howard   125, 126
Taylor, Zachery   119
Thanksgiving   53–54
Thrushes   139
Trick-or-treating   68–69, 71–72
Tumbleweeds   46
Turkeys   63–64
Tyler, John   125

UNIVAC I   123–124

Vampire bats   90–91

Warblers   139
Washington, Geroge   54, 118, 125
Wasps
   hibernation   148
   mud-dauber wasps   146
Weasel   144
Whigs   119
Whitney, Eli   39–40
Wildflowers   17–22
Willet, William   3–4
Wilson, Woodrow   120
Wisteria   50
Witches   79–80
Wizards   79
Wolverines   89–90

Yom Kippur   107

Zuni   71